3

Contemporary Topics

21st Century Skills for Academic Success

FOURTH EDITION

David Beglar • Neil Murray

Michael Rost
SERIES EDITOR

Contemporary Topics 3, **Advanced**
21st Century Skills for Academic Success
Fourth Edition

Copyright © 2017 by Pearson Education, Inc. or its affiliates.

Pearson Education, 221 River Street, Hoboken, NJ 07030

Staff credits: The people who made up the *Contemporary Topics* team, representing editorial, production, design, and manufacturing are Pietro Alongi, Claire Bowers, Stephanie Bullard, Kim Casey, Tracey Cataldo, Mindy DePalma, Dave Dickey, Pam Fishman, Niki Lee, Fabrizio Luccitti, Amy McCormick, Jennifer Raspiller, Robert Ruvo, Leigh Stolle, Paula Van Ells, and Joseph Vella.

Cover image: © Fotolia/Suchota
Text composition: MPS North America
Photo credits: See page 134

Library of Congress Cataloging-in-Publication Data
A catalog record for the print edition is available from the Library of Congress
ISBN-10: 0-13-440079-8   ISBN-13: 978-0-13-440079-2

Printed in the United States of America.
4   17

Contents

Scope and Sequence

UNIT SUBJECT AND TITLE	CORPUS-BASED VOCABULARY	NOTE-TAKING AND LISTENING FOCUS	PRONUNCIATION	DISCUSSION STRATEGY	PRESENTATION
1 COMMUNICATION STUDIES Slang and Language Change	attitudes constantly construct evolving expanding identity inevitable phenomenon reinforce widespread	Sequence markers to organize your notes	Contractions	• **Paraphrasing** • Agreeing • Asking for clarification or confirmation	Present about language after conducting effective research
2 CHILD PSYCHOLOGY The Genius Within	devote exhibit inconsistencies motivation predominant strategy underlying	Examples	Glides	• **Offering a fact or example** • Asking for clarification or confirmation • Asking for opinions or ideas	Present on giftedness while considering the audience
3 SOCIOLOGY Online Communities	access contribute generate indicate investment obtain potential	Key terms and definitions	Thought groups	• **Keeping a discussion on topic** • Asking for opinions or ideas • Expressing an opinion	Present on social networking after using various practice techniques
4 BUSINESS Core Business Skills	acquire diverse intelligence occupation prioritize	Symbols and abbreviations	Sounds influencing -s	• **Bringing a discussion to a close** • Expressing an opinion • Offering a fact or example	Present on a core business skill, using organization techniques
5 COGNITIVE PSYCHOLOGY Memory	chemicals decade implicit logical manipulate psychologist release retain temporarily	Cause-and-effect relationships	Sounds influencing -t	• **Getting a discussion started** • Keeping a discussion on topic • Offering a fact or example	Present on enhancing memory while connecting with the audience
6 ANTHROPOLOGY/ BIOLOGY The Science of Love	attachment enhance invoke mutual prospective	Lists	Reduced words and disappearing sounds	• **Disagreeing** • Asking for opinions or ideas • Trying to reach a consensus	Present on a topic related to love, using presentation management techniques

UNIT SUBJECT AND TITLE	CORPUS-BASED VOCABULARY	NOTE-TAKING AND LISTENING FOCUS	PRONUNCIATION	DISCUSSION STRATEGY	PRESENTATION
7 TECHNOLOGY Artificial Intelligence: The Turning Point	awareness complex equivalent implication rationally reactionary reliable	Organization	Syllable stress	• **Asking for opinions or ideas** • Expressing an opinion • Offering a fact or example	Present on the advantages and disadvantages of a new AI technology, working as part of a team
8 POLITICAL SCIENCE Big Brother and the Surveillance Society	civil controversial security technique via	Numbers and statistics	Key words in thought groups	• **Trying to reach a consensus** • Asking for clarification or confirmation • Expressing an opinion	Present on the issues of surveillance and privacy, using a slideshow
9 LINGUISTICS Animal Communication	discrete distinct flexible generation precise random ultimately	Comparisons and contrasts	Key word stress	• **Expressing an opinion** • Agreeing • Asking for clarification or confirmation	Present on the communication habits of an animal, using visual data
10 ECONOMICS The Evolution of Money	abandon abstract currency enormous initiative undergo	Notations	Linking	• **Agreeing** • Expressing an opinion • Offering a fact or example	Present on money and answer audience questions
11 BIOLOGY The Fountain of Youth	accumulate benefit function plus supplement	Problem-solution relationships	Verb forms	• **Asking for clarification or confirmation** • Asking for opinions or ideas • Disagreeing	Present on slowing the aging process while creating group interactions
12 SOCIOLOGY Marriage	adulthood confirm couple matured norm	Personal reactions to topics	Discourse markers	• **Offering an example or idea** • Expressing an opinion • Paraphrasing	Present on an aspect of marriage and ask rhetorical questions

Acknowledgments

The series editor, authors, and publisher would like to thank the following consultants, reviewers, and teachers for offering their invaluable insights and suggestions for the fourth edition of the *Contemporary Topics* series.

Kate Reynolds, *University of Wisconsin-Eau Claire*; Kathie Gerecke, *North Shore Community College*; Jeanne Dunnett, *Central Connecticut State University*; Linda Anderson, *Washington University in St. Louis/Fontbonne University*; Sande Wu, *California State University, Fresno*; Stephanie Landon, *College of the Desert*; Jungsook Kim, *Jeungsang Language School*; Jenny Oh Kim, *Kangnamgu Daechidong*; Patty Heiser, *University of Washington*; Carrie Barnard, *Queens College*; Lori D. Giles, *University of Miami*; Nancy H. Centers, *Roger Williams University*; Lyra Riabov, *Southern New Hampshire University*; Dr. Steven Gras, *ESL Program, SUNY Plattsburgh*; series consultants Jeanette Clement and Cynthia Lennox, *Duquesne University*

New to this fourth edition, **Essential Online Resources** are available at **www.pearsonelt.com/contemporarytopics4e**, using your access code. These resources include the following:

- **VIDEO:** Watch the Lecture academic lecture videos, with or without Presentation Points, and Talk About the Topic student discussion videos are available.
- **AUDIO:** Audio clips for all audio-based Student Book activities as well as Unit Tests and Proficiency Assessment lectures are available. Audio versions of the unit lectures and student discussion are also provided. (Audio and video icons in the Student Book and Teaching Tips indicate which media is needed for each activity.)
- **STUDENT BOOK PRESENTATION SLIDES:** All units of the Student Book are available as PowerPoint® slides, allowing activities to be viewed as a class.
- **INTERACTIVE TESTS:** Teachers can administer the Unit Tests and Proficiency Assessments online.
- **PRINT RESOURCES:** Transcripts of the videos and lecture-specific Coaching Tips (covering listening, critical thinking, and note-taking) are provided along with Teaching Tips, Answer Keys, Audioscripts, Teacher and Student Evaluations Forms, Unit Tests, and Proficiency Assessments.

Introduction

The *Contemporary Topics* series provides a comprehensive approach to developing 21st century academic skills—including listening, thinking, discussion, presentation, and study skills—in order to prepare students for participation in real-life academic and professional contexts.

The overriding principle of language and skill development in the *Contemporary Topics* series is *engagement*. Activities in each unit are carefully sequenced in a way that gives students increasing involvement and self-direction of their learning. Authentic, stimulating content is introduced and developed throughout each unit so that students experience the value of understanding and exchanging contemporary ideas in a range of academic fields. *Contemporary Topics* is intended to bridge the gap between language-focused and content-focused instruction, to ready students for genuine academic and professional contexts where they will be expected to participate fully.

Each unit centers around a short academic lecture. Realistic preparation activities, focused listening tasks, personalized discussions, challenging tests, and authentic presentation assignments enable students to explore each topic deeply.

The lecture topics are drawn from a range of academic disciplines, and the lectures themselves feature engaging instructors in a variety of settings including offices, lecture halls, and classrooms, many with live student audiences.

In order to achieve the goals of content-based instruction, the *Contemporary Topics* series has developed an engaging nine-part learning methodology:

Section 1: Connect to the Topic
Estimated time: 15 minutes
This opening section invites students to activate what they already know about the unit topic by connecting the topic to their personal experiences and beliefs. Typically, students fill out a short survey and compare answers with a partner. The students then listen to a short interview providing one expert view on the unit topic. The teacher then acts as a facilitator for students to share some of their initial ideas about the topic before they explore it further.

Section 2: Build Your Vocabulary
Estimated time: 15 minutes
This section familiarizes students with some of the key content words and phrases used in the lecture. Each lecture targets 10–15 key words from the Academic Word List to ensure that students learn the core vocabulary needed for academic success.

Students read *and listen* to the target words and phrases in context so that they can better prepare for the upcoming lecture. Students then work individually or with a partner to complete exercises to ensure an initial understanding of the target lexis of the unit. A supplementary pair-work activity enables students to focus on form as they are learning new words and collocations.

Section 3: Focus Your Attention
Estimated time: 10 minutes
In this section, students learn strategies for listening actively and taking clear notes. Because a major part of "active listening" involves a readiness to deal with comprehension difficulties, this section provides specific coaching tips to help students direct their attention and gain more control of how they listen.

Tips include how to use signal words as organization cues, make lists, note definitions, link examples to main ideas, identify causes and effects, and separate points of view. A Try It section, based on a short audio extract, allows students to work on note-taking strategies before they get to the main lecture. Examples of actual notes are usually provided in this section to give students concrete "starter models" they can use in the classroom.

Section 4: Watch the Lecture

Estimated time: 20–30 minutes

As the central section of each unit, Watch the Lecture allows for two full listening cycles, one to focus on "top-down listening" strategies (Listen for Main Ideas) and one to focus on "bottom-up listening" strategies (Listen for Details).

In keeping with the principles of content-based instruction, students are provided with several layers of support. In the Think About It section, students are guided to activate concepts and vocabulary they have studied earlier in the unit.

The lecture can be viewed as a video or just listened to on audio. The video version includes the speaker's Presentation Points.

Section 5: Hear the Language

Estimated time: 10 minutes

This section focuses on "bottom-up" listening strategies and pronunciation. In this section, students hear ten short extracts taken from the actual lecture and perform a noticing task. The task helps students perceive sound reductions and assimilations, learn to hear language as "thought groups" and pauses, and tune in to function of stress and intonation.

Students then work in pairs to practice their pronunciation, adapting the phonology point that was learned in the listening task.

Section 6: Talk About the Topic

Estimated time: 15 minutes

Here students gain valuable discussion skills as they talk about the content of the lectures. Discussion skills are an important part of academic success, and most students benefit from structured practice with these skills. In this activity, students first listen to a short "model discussion" involving native and nonnative speakers, and identify the speaking strategies and gambits that are used. They then attempt to use some of those strategies in their own discussion groups.

The discussion strategies modeled and explained across the units include the following:

- Agreeing
- Asking for clarification or confirmation
- Asking for opinions or ideas
- Disagreeing
- Expressing an opinion
- Keeping a discussion on topic
- Offering a fact or example
- Trying to reach a consensus
- Paraphrasing

Section 7: Review Your Notes

Estimated time: 10 minutes

Using notes for review and discussion is an important study skill that is developed in this section. Research has shown that the value of note-taking for memory building is realized *primarily* when note-takers review their notes and attempt to reconstruct the content.

In this activity, students are guided in reviewing the content of the unit, clarifying concepts, and preparing for the Unit Test. Abbreviated examples of actual notes are provided to help students compare and improve their own note-taking skills.

Section 8: Take the Unit Test and Proficiency Assessment

Estimated time: 15 minutes each

Taking the **Unit Test** completes the study cycle of the unit: preparation for the lecture, listening to the lecture, review of the content, and assessment.

The Unit Test, contained only in the Teacher's Pack, is administered by the teacher and then completed in class, using the accompanying audio. The tests in *Contemporary Topics* are intended to be challenging—to motivate students to learn the material thoroughly. The format features an answer sheet with choices. The question "stem" is provided on audio only. Test-taking skills include verbatim recall, paraphrasing, inferencing, and synthesizing information from different parts of the lecture.

The **Proficiency Assessment** is an audio lecture and ten multiple-choice questions designed to give students practice listening and taking standardized tests. It, too, is found only in the Teacher's Pack and should be administered by the teacher and completed in class using the accompanying audio.

Section 9: Express Your Ideas

Estimated time: Will vary by class size

This final section creates a natural extension of the unit topic to areas that are relevant to students. Students go through a guided process of preparing, practicing, and presenting on a topic of personal interest. Students are also given guidance in listening to other students' presentations and providing helpful feedback.

A supplementary Teacher's Pack (TP) contains teaching tips, transcripts, answer keys, tests, and teacher evaluation forms.

We hope you will enjoy using this course. While the *Contemporary Topics* series provides an abundance of learning activities and media, the key to making the course work in your classroom is student engagement and commitment. For content-based learning to be effective, students need to become *active* learners. This involves thinking critically, guessing, interacting, offering ideas, collaborating, questioning, and responding. The authors and editors of *Contemporary Topics* have created a rich framework for encouraging students to become active, successful learners. We hope that we have also provided you, the teacher, with tools for becoming an active guide to the students in their learning.

Michael Rost
SERIES EDITOR

Learning Path

ACTIVATION SECTIONS 1 / 2 / 3

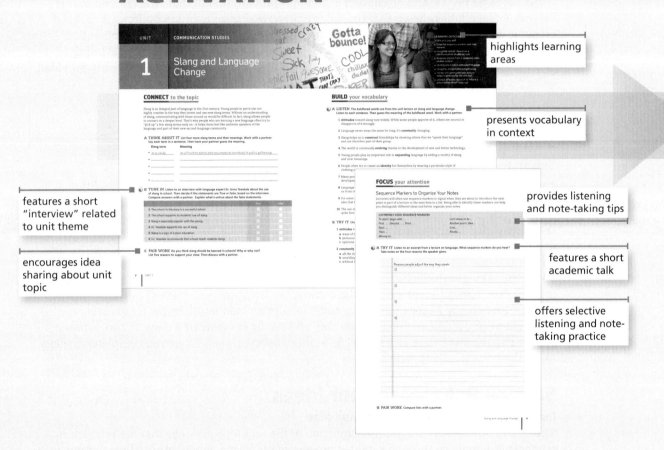

highlights learning areas

presents vocabulary in context

features a short "interview" related to unit theme

provides listening and note-taking tips

features a short academic talk

encourages idea sharing about unit topic

offers selective listening and note-taking practice

EXPRESSION SECTION 9

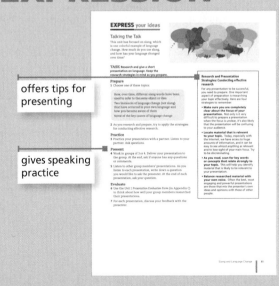

offers tips for presenting

gives speaking practice

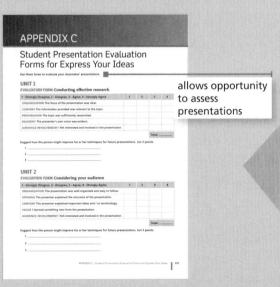

allows opportunity to assess presentations

PROCESSING SECTIONS 4 / 5 / 6

encourages anticipation of lecture topic

features an academic lecture and requires gist and intensive listening, and active note-taking

features lecture extracts that demonstrate phonology points

prompts pronunciation practice

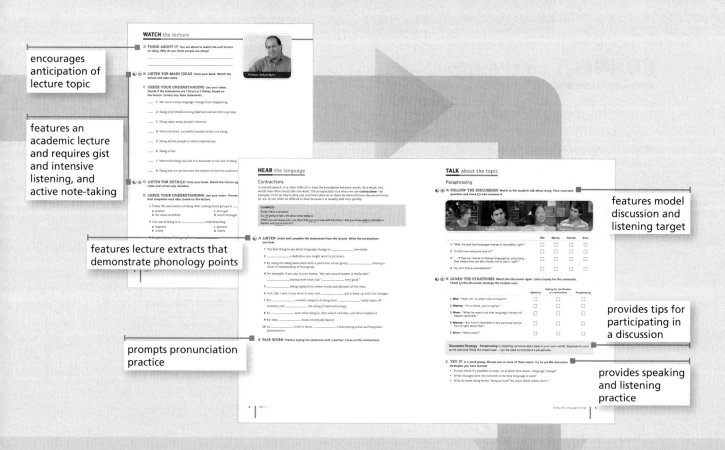

features model discussion and listening target

provides tips for participating in a discussion

provides speaking and listening practice

ASSESSMENT SECTIONS 7 / 8

provides opportunity to revise notes

allows demonstration of content mastery

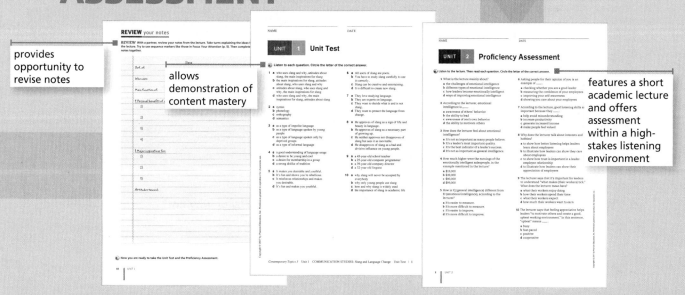

features a short academic lecture and offers assessment within a high-stakes listening environment

1 Slang and Language Change

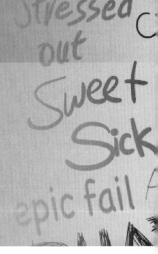

CONNECT to the topic

Slang is an integral part of language in the 21st century. Young people in particular are highly creative in the way they invent and use new slang terms. Without an understanding of slang, communicating with those around us would be difficult. In fact, slang allows people to connect on a deeper level. That's why people who are learning a new language often try to "pick up" a few slang terms early on—it helps them feel like authentic speakers of the language and part of their new second-language community.

A THINK ABOUT IT List four more slang terms and their meanings. Work with a partner. Say each term in a sentence. Then have your partner guess the meaning.

Slang term	Meaning
• arm candy	an attractive person who accompanies somebody to public gatherings
• _____	_____
• _____	_____
• _____	_____
• _____	_____

B TUNE IN Listen to an interview with language expert Dr. Anna Teesdale about the use of slang in school. Then decide if the statements are *True* or *False*, based on the interview. Compare answers with a partner. Explain what's untrue about the false statements.

	True	False
1 The school in the story is a successful school.	☐	☐
2 The school supports its students' use of slang.	☐	☐
3 Slang is especially popular with the young.	☐	☐
4 Dr. Teesdale supports the use of slang.	☐	☐
5 Slang is a sign of a poor education.	☐	☐
6 Dr. Teesdale recommends that schools teach students slang.	☐	☐

C PAIR WORK Do you think slang should be banned in schools? Why or why not? List five reasons to support your view. Then discuss with a partner.

BUILD your vocabulary

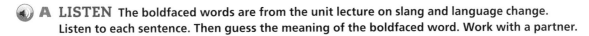

A LISTEN The boldfaced words are from the unit lecture on slang and language change. Listen to each sentence. Then guess the meaning of the boldfaced word. Work with a partner.

1 **Attitudes** toward slang vary widely. While some people approve of it, others are neutral or disapprove of it strongly.

2 Language never stays the same for long; it's **constantly** changing.

3 Slang helps us to **construct** friendships by showing others that we "speak their language" and are therefore part of their group.

4 The world is continually **evolving** thanks to the development of new and better technology.

5 Young people play an important role in **expanding** language by adding a variety of slang and new meanings.

6 People often try to create an **identity** for themselves by wearing a particular style of clothing or speaking in a certain way.

7 Many people think that a desire to be different is an **inevitable** part of teenage development, a natural phase teens can't avoid.

8 Language is a fascinating and unique **phenomenon**. How human language distinguishes us from other animals has been studied for years.

9 For some people, teenagers' use of slang and other forms of "bad" language **reinforces** the idea that they are rebellious and do not want to conform.

10 The use of slang was not always as **widespread** as it is today; nowadays most people use it quite freely.

B TRY IT Choose the best definition for each boldfaced word.

1 **attitudes** vary
  a ways of behaving
  b personalities
  c opinions and feelings

2 **constantly** change
  a all the time
  b unwillingly
  c without thinking

3 **construct** friendships
  a search for
  b create or build
  c understand the meaning of

4 continually **evolving**
  a developing
  b becoming worse
  c going out of fashion

5 expanding language

   a showing off
   b checking
   c increasing

6 create an **identity**

   a facial expression
   b quality that makes someone distinct
   c sense of interest

7 an **inevitable** part

   a unavoidable
   b important
   c difficult

8 a **phenomenon**

   a human characteristic
   b remarkable thing
   c idea

9 reinforces the idea

   a devalues
   b supports
   c creates

10 not as **widespread** as

   a important
   b popular
   c common

C PAIR WORK Cover Group A as your partner reads sentences 1–5. Listen and write the missing words in Group B. Your partner corrects your answers. Switch roles for 6–10.

GROUP A

1 People always try to **adapt to** their communities.

2 Slang **breeds in** groups who don't want to be understood.

3 We show our beliefs **by using** particular language.

4 Slang is **the focus of** a lot of language research.

5 Many parents aren't **in tune with** their teenagers' interests.

6 New language tends to be closely **associated with** youth.

7 Some slang is **exclusive to** particular communities.

8 **Experts in** language are often fascinated by slang.

9 Language is crucial to our **integration into** society.

10 Some social groups are **made distinct by** their unique use of language.

GROUP B

1 People always try to **adapt** _____ their communities.

2 Slang **breeds** _____ groups who don't want to be understood.

3 We show our beliefs _____ **using** particular language.

4 Slang is **the focus** _____ a lot of language research.

5 Many parents aren't **in tune** _____ their teenagers' interests.

6 New language tends to be closely **associated** _____ youth.

7 Some slang is **exclusive** _____ particular communities.

8 **Experts** _____ language are often fascinated by slang.

9 Language is crucial to our **integration** _____ society.

10 Some social groups are **made distinct** _____ their unique use of language.

FOCUS your attention

Sequence Markers to Organize Your Notes

Lecturers will often use sequence markers to signal when they are about to introduce the next point or part of a lecture or the next item in a list. Being able to identify these markers can help you distinguish different ideas and better organize your notes.

COMMONLY USED SEQUENCE MARKERS	
To start / begin with, ...	*Let's move on to ...*
First, ... ; Second, ... ; Third, ...	*Another point / idea ...*
Next, ...	*Last, ...*
Then ...	*Finally, ...*
Moving on ...	

A TRY IT Listen to an excerpt from a lecture on language. What sequence markers do you hear? Take notes on the four reasons the speaker gives.

Reasons people adjust the way they speak:

1)

2)

3)

4)

B PAIR WORK Compare lists with a partner.

WATCH the lecture

A THINK ABOUT IT You are about to watch the unit lecture on slang. Why do you think people use slang?

_____

_____

Professor Robert Myers

B LISTEN FOR MAIN IDEAS Close your book. Watch the lecture and take notes.

C CHECK YOUR UNDERSTANDING Use your notes. Decide if the statements are *T* (true) or *F* (false), based on the lecture. Correct any false statements.

_____ **1** We cannot stop language change from happening.

_____ **2** Slang only breeds among deprived and secretive groups.

_____ **3** Slang takes away people's identity.

_____ **4** Well-educated, successful people rarely use slang.

_____ **5** Slang allows people to share experiences.

_____ **6** Slang is fun.

_____ **7** New technology has led to a decrease in the use of slang.

_____ **8** Slang has not yet become the subject of serious academic study.

D LISTEN FOR DETAILS Close your book. Watch the lecture again. Add details to your notes and correct any mistakes.

E CHECK YOUR UNDERSTANDING Use your notes. Choose the word or phrase that best completes each idea, based on the lecture.

1 Today the association of slang with underground groups is _____ .
- **a** weaker
- **b** the same as before
- **c** stronger
- **d** much stronger

2 One use of slang is to _____ understanding.
- **a** improve
- **b** create
- **c** prevent
- **d** check

3 People who are "out-group" are _____ .
- **a** excluded
- **b** respected
- **c** opponents of slang
- **d** poor users of slang

4 Slang can give people status if they _____ .

  a know the latest slang terms   **c** avoid bad slang

  b use it frequently   **d** know how to use it

5 S.I. Hayakawa describes slang as "the poetry of everyday _____ ."

  a love   **c** emotions

  b life   **d** feelings and beliefs

6 One of the richest sources of slang today is _____ .

  a love and romance   **c** new technology

  b expressions of like and dislike   **d** websites about slang

7 According to the lecture, slang _____ considered taboo.

  a used to be   **c** is still

  b was never   **d** is increasingly

8 People who dislike slang often associate it with groups who are _____

and _____ .

  a uneducated / criminal   **c** impolite / uneducated

  b criminal / undesirable   **d** undesirable / uneducated

9 People who see themselves as "guardians" of a language feel that changes

make it _____ .

  a worse   **c** full of slang

  b better   **d** more creative

10 The lecturer's attitude toward language change is _____ .

  a extremely negative   **c** neutral

  b negative   **d** positive

HEAR the language

Contractions

In natural speech, it is often difficult to hear the boundaries between words. As a result, two words may often sound like one word. This is especially true when we use **contractions**—for example, it's (it is), they're (they are), and here's (here is). In these shortened forms, the second word (is, are, is) can often be difficult to hear because it is usually said very quickly.

EXAMPLES

Study these examples:

So I'm going to talk a bit about what slang is.

When you use slang well, you show that you're in tune with the times—that you know what's culturally in fashion and you're part of it.

A LISTEN Listen and complete the statements from the lecture. Write the contractions you hear.

1 The first thing to say about language change is _____ inevitable.

2 _____ a definition you might want to jot down.

3 By using the slang associated with a particular social group, _____ staking a claim to membership of that group.

4 For example, if you say to your friend, "My new sound system is really safe,"

_____ saying more than just "_____ very good."

5 _____ being replaced by newer words and phrases all the time.

6 And, like I said, if you want to stay cool, _____ got to keep up with the changes.

7 But _____ another category of slang term _____ really taken off

recently, and _____ the slang of new technology.

8 So, _____ seen what slang is, who uses it and why, and what inspires it.

9 But that _____ mean everybody likes it.

10 As _____ tried to show, _____ a fascinating social and linguistic phenomenon.

B PAIR WORK Practice saying the sentences with a partner. Focus on the contractions.

TALK about the topic

Paraphrasing

A FOLLOW THE DISCUSSION Watch as the students talk about slang. Then read each question and check (√) who answers it.

Mia *Manny* *Hannah* *River*

	Mia	Manny	Hannah	River
1 "Well, he said that language change is inevitable, right?"	☐	☐	☐	☐
2 "Is that how everyone took it?"	☐	☐	☐	☐
3 " … If they can choose to change language by using slang, that means they can also choose not to use it, right?"	☐	☐	☐	☐
4 "So, isn't that a contradiction?"	☐	☐	☐	☐

B LEARN THE STRATEGIES Watch the discussion again. Listen closely for the comments. Check (√) the discussion strategy the student uses.

	Agreeing	Asking for clarification or confirmation	Paraphrasing
1 **Mia:** "Yeah, OK. So what's the confusion?"	☐	☐	☐
2 **Manny:** "It's a choice, you're saying."	☐	☐	☐
3 **River:** "What he meant was that language change will happen generally."	☐	☐	☐
4 **Manny:** "But it isn't inevitable in any particular group … You're right about that."	☐	☐	☐
5 **River:** "Make sense?"	☐	☐	☐

Discussion Strategy **Paraphrasing** is restating someone else's idea in your own words. Expressions such as *He said* and *What she meant was …* can be used to introduce a paraphrase.

C TRY IT In a small group, discuss one or more of these topics. Try to use the discussion strategies you have learned.

- Do you think it's possible to stop—or at least slow down—language change?
- What changes have you noticed in the way language is used?
- Why do some slang terms "hang around" for years while others don't?

REVIEW your notes

REVIEW With a partner, review your notes from the lecture. Take turns explaining the ideas from the lecture. Try to use sequence markers like those in Focus Your Attention (p. 5). Then complete these notes together.

Slang

Def. of:

Who uses:

Main function of:

4 Personal benefits of using:

   1)

   2)

   3)

   4)

3 Major inspirations for:

   1)

   2)

   3)

Attitudes toward:

Now you are ready to take the Unit Test and the Proficiency Assessment.

EXPRESS your ideas

Talking the Talk

This unit has focused on slang, which is one colorful example of language change. How much do you use slang, and how has your language changed over time?

TASK Research and give a short presentation on language. Keep the research strategies in mind as you prepare.

Prepare

1 Choose one of these topics:

> How, over time, different slang words have been used to refer to the same object or idea
>
> Two instances of language change (not slang) that have occurred in your own language and how you became aware of them
>
> Some of the key causes of language change

2 As you research and prepare, try to apply the strategies for conducting effective research.

Practice

3 Practice your presentation with a partner. Listen to your partner. Ask questions.

Present

4 Work in groups of 3 or 4. Deliver your presentation to the group. At the end, ask if anyone has any questions or comments.

5 Listen to other group members' presentations. As you listen to each presentation, write down a question you would like to ask the presenter. At the end of each presentation, ask your question.

Evaluate

6 Use the *Unit 1 Presentation Evaluation Form* (in Appendix C) to think about how well your group members researched their presentations.

7 For each presentation, discuss your feedback with the presenter.

Research and Presentation Strategies: Conducting effective research

For any presentation to be successful, you need to prepare. One important aspect of preparation is researching your topic effectively. Here are four strategies to remember:

- **Make sure you are completely clear about the focus of your presentation.** Not only is it very difficult to prepare a presentation when the focus is unclear, it's also likely that the presentation will be confusing to your audience.

- **Locate material that is relevant to your topic.** Today, especially with the Internet, we have access to huge amounts of information, and it can be easy to see *almost anything* as relevant and to lose sight of your main focus. Try to be discriminating.

- **As you read, scan for key words or concepts that relate strongly to your topic.** This will help you identify material that is likely to be relevant to your presentation.

- **Balance researched material with your own voice.** Often the best, most engaging and powerful presentations are those that mix the presenter's own ideas and opinions with those of other people.

2   The Genius Within

CONNECT to the topic

Although there is no universally agreed-upon definition of what a gifted child is, all cultures recognize that some children are special. These children seem to have a natural talent that allows them to perform in ways that are far beyond their physical age. By the age of three or four, they may have an ear for music, a talent for drawing, or a flair for performing. In other cases, their gift becomes apparent when they begin school and surprise their teachers with their understanding of mathematics, science, or literature.

A THINK ABOUT IT Take this survey about giftedness. Check (✓) your responses and think of reasons or examples to support them. Then compare with a partner.

	Agree	Disagree
• Many children are gifted.	☐	☐
• I know a gifted person.	☐	☐
• Most successful adults were gifted children.	☐	☐
• You don't need to have natural ability to be gifted.	☐	☐
• It's always an advantage to be gifted.	☐	☐

B TUNE IN Listen to an interview with the father of a gifted child, Lionel Driscol. Then circle the best answer, based on the interview. Compare answers with a partner.

1 Gifted children can undermine parents' **relationships / confidence / happiness**.

2 Driscol and his wife realized their daughter was gifted when she was **eight / fifteen / eighteen** months old.

3 Marianne has difficulty **studying / socializing / playing sports** with other children.

4 Asynchronous development is when a child's mental age and physical age **match / don't match**.

5 Gifted children often don't sleep well because their brains are very **active / uncontrolled / stressed**.

6 Mensa has been a **positive / negative** experience for Marianne and her parents.

C PAIR WORK List at least three ways that children can be gifted. Provide an example for each. Then discuss with a partner.

LEARNING OUTCOMES
In this unit you will:

- extract examples from a short talk
- restate the main ideas of a child psychology lecture
- fact-check statements about a child psychology lecture
- identify and practice linked words
- recognize and practice offering a fact or example
- review with a partner to prepare for the unit test
- research and present on giftedness while considering the audience

BUILD your vocabulary

A LISTEN The boldfaced words are from the unit lecture on gifted children. Listen to each sentence. Then choose the meaning of the boldfaced word.

1 Saki is unusually **alert** for a six-month-old baby. She seems to notice everything around her.
   a behaving very stubbornly
   b smiling and laughing happily
   c watching and listening carefully

2 Zoe has an **aptitude** for sports. She learns very quickly and very well.
   a a special quality that makes other people like her
   b a behavior intended to make other people laugh
   c a natural ability or skill

3 Carlos has **devoted** himself to learning how to play the cello.
   a given a feeling of great pleasure
   b asked strongly for something
   c given time and perhaps money to some activity

4 Some children **exhibit** extraordinary talent at a young age.
   a show something so that it's easy to notice
   b get something through hard work
   c do something to entertain people

5 Children with a good **imagination** can write interesting stories.
   a the ability to focus on one thing intensely
   b the ability to form creative ideas in your mind
   c a work area that has many types of tools

6 I noticed several **inconsistencies** in his words and behavior.
   a two or more pieces of information that do not agree with one another
   b positive personal characteristics
   c actions that are done to help others

7 Most children have a natural **motivation** to explore the world around them.

    a an opinion about something
    b an action taken to deal with a problem
    c eagerness and willingness to do something

8 A **predominant** characteristic of most children is that they are curious about the world.

    a more powerful than others
    b more harmful than others
    c more controlling than others

9 One learning **strategy** that some talented children use is to do the same activity in several different ways.

    a a way of talking
    b a school where students are very physically active
    c a plan used to achieve a goal

10 Once we discover the **underlying** principles of an event, we can understand why it happens.

    a mistaken or wrong
    b hidden and not easy to discover
    c strange and unexpected

B **PAIR WORK** With a partner, reorder the words to make complete sentences.
Notice the boldfaced words. Then take turns saying the sentences. Review any words you don't understand.

  1 People often (gifted / a / of / **think** / as / child) when that child learns extremely quickly.

  2 Michelle's (dance **aptitude** / apparent / became / **for**) when she was about six years old.

  3 I think that (underlying / understand / **for** / the / I / **reasons**) his reluctance to join the team.

  4 Some children seem to have (an / **for** / mathematics / **ability** / innate / doing).

  5 Greta can write interesting stories (**because** / unusually / of / imagination / her / creative).

  6 Miguel (has / lot **time** / **devoted /** a / of) **to** learning French this year.

  7 Intelligent children tend to be (the / somewhat / **about** / people / **idealistic**) who they know.

  8 Most intelligent children are observant; (they / many / notice / **about** / **details**) their environment.

  9 As children learn how the world works, (**about** / can / they / **predictions** / **make**) what will probably happen next.

  10 Because they encourage deeper thinking, (are / **than** / strategies / **some** / effective / **more** / **others**).

FOCUS your attention

Examples

Lecturers will sometimes give examples in order to illustrate a point. These examples are important because they make abstract ideas more concrete and understandable. They may also help you remember the abstract idea.

> **WAYS LECTURERS MIGHT PRESENT AN EXAMPLE**
>
> *For example ...*
> *For instance ...*
> *... such as ...*
> *An example of this is ...*
> *One example would be ...*
> *Let me give you an example of this.*

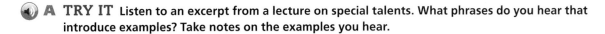 **A TRY IT** Listen to an excerpt from a lecture on special talents. What phrases do you hear that introduce examples? Take notes on the examples you hear.

Special talents

Examples:

B PAIR WORK Compare notes with a partner.

WATCH the lecture

Professor Nadine Clarke

A THINK ABOUT IT You are about to watch the unit lecture on gifted children. How do you think gifted children are identified?

_____

_____

B LISTEN FOR MAIN IDEAS Close your book. Watch the lecture and take notes.

C CHECK YOUR UNDERSTANDING Use your notes. Complete the main ideas, based on the lecture.

1 The first way gifted children are identified is that they show _____ .
   a enjoyment doing a skill
   b interest in a skill
   c above-average ability

2 Some psychologists believe that _____ is perhaps the best indicator of giftedness.
   a speed of learning
   b quality of performance
   c number of mistakes

3 One common personality characteristic of gifted children is their _____ .
   a cheerfulness
   b intensity
   c verbal ability

4 Another common personality characteristic of gifted children is that they are often _____ .
   a idealistic
   b pessimistic
   c focused on the present

5 Gifted children often don't care about the _____ of the knowledge or skill that they are learning.
   a difficulty
   b usefulness
   c popularity

6 When studying something new, gifted children are very interested in

   _____ .

   a telling others what they have learned
   b the cause-and-effect relationship
   c using their new knowledge

🔊 ▶ **D LISTEN FOR DETAILS** Close your book. Watch the lecture again. Add details to your notes and correct any mistakes.

E CHECK YOUR UNDERSTANDING Use your notes. Decide if the statements are *T* (true) or *F* (false), based on the lecture. Correct any false statements.

_____ **1** Gifted children show strong ability in something, particularly considering their age.

_____ **2** Gifted children generally make the same number of mistakes as other children.

_____ **3** Many gifted children have difficulty concentrating for long periods of time.

_____ **4** Most gifted children have a great deal of mental energy, but normal levels of emotional energy.

_____ **5** Gifted children notice many details about the things they are interested in.

_____ **6** Gifted children use their knowledge of underlying principles to make predictions.

_____ **7** Gifted children generally have very good learning strategies.

HEAR the language

Glides

In conversational speech, English speakers will often connect the final sound of one word to the initial sound of the following word. This typically introduces a linking sound, called a **glide**, such as the y sound in be**y**able (be able) and the w sound in do**w**it (do it). Glides such as these make speakers sound more fluent, but they can also make listening more difficult.

> **EXAMPLES**
>
> Notice how the final sound of the first underlined word influences the initial sound in the next word:
>
> *Gifted children appear to be **i**ntensely curious about every topic.*
>
> *The have very good learning strategies that we can learn **to u**se.*

A LISTEN Listen and complete the statements and questions from the lecture. Each sentence has a pair of words that is linked with a glide. Write the individual words.

1 Let me begin _____ by _____ asking _____ you to think about someone you believe is exceptionally talented.

2 Well, today I'd like to talk about children who are very talented, children often referred _____ to _____ Has _____ "gifted."

3 Now, how would _____ you _____ idntify _____ a gifted child?

4 I'm sure that you knew some students _____ who _____ exuabited _____ exceptional talents.

5 Well, _____ see _____ of _____ these ideas make sense to you.

6 So when we _____ see _____ a _____ very young child who shows above-average athletic ability, for example, we often conclude that the child has an innate ability for sports.

7 When they do something, especially something they enjoy, they devote all their energy and determination _____ to _____ it _____ .

8 In other words, they want to know _____ the _____ undeline _____ principles and use those principles for making generalizations and predictions about the thing they are studying.

9 Gifted children are motivated, they are alert and observant, they concentrate intensely, they try _____ to _____ understand _____ cause-and-effect relationships, and they make an effort to think creatively.

10 How well could _____ you _____ and _____ I learn to do something if we approached it like I've just described?

B PAIR WORK Practice saying each pair of linked words with a partner. Say them in isolation by pronouncing the glides. Then practice saying the complete sentence, focusing on the glides.

TALK about the topic

Offering a Fact or Example

A FOLLOW THE DISCUSSION Watch as the students talk about the roles of practice and innate talent in genius. Then read each opinion and check (√) who agrees with it. More than one student may agree.

Yhinny   Michael   May   Qiang

	Yhinny	Michael	May	Qiang
1 The instructor didn't emphasize the importance of innate talents enough.	☐	☐	☐	☑
2 Mozart and Emily Dickinson were naturally talented.	☑	☐	☑	☑
3 Hard work is as important as innate abilities.	☑	☐	☑	☐

B LEARN THE STRATEGIES Watch the discussion again. Listen closely for the comments. Check (√) the discussion strategy the student uses.

	Asking for clarification or confirmation	Asking for opinions or ideas	Offering a fact or example
1 **Yhinny:** "You have to study something or practice something really hard for either 10,000 hours or 10 years to become really great at something."	☐	☐	☑
2 **May:** "Like, talents that we're born with?"	☑	☐	☐
3 **Qiang:** "I mean, look at Mozart and his innate talent for music. Or Emily Dickinson and her innate talent for literature."	☐	☐	☑
4 **May:** "I mean, Mozart, he practiced for hours! His father forced him."	☐	☐	☑
5 **Michael:** "So how do I identify a gifted child?"	☐	☑	☐

Discussion Strategy   To bolster your idea or position on an issue, you can **offer a fact or example** as support. Facts and examples—such as statistics, dates, and historic events—not only add richness to the discussion but also increase your credibility as a speaker.

C TRY IT In a small group, discuss one or more of these topics. Try to use the discussion strategies you have learned.

- Do you agree with the 10,000-hour, 10-year rule of genius?
- Qiang argues that innate talent is the most important part of genius. Do you agree?
- How can people motivate themselves to practice a skill for many years?

REVIEW your notes

REVIEW With a partner, review your notes from the lecture. Take turns explaining the ideas from the lecture, using the headings below to help you. Give examples as you discuss. Then complete these notes together.

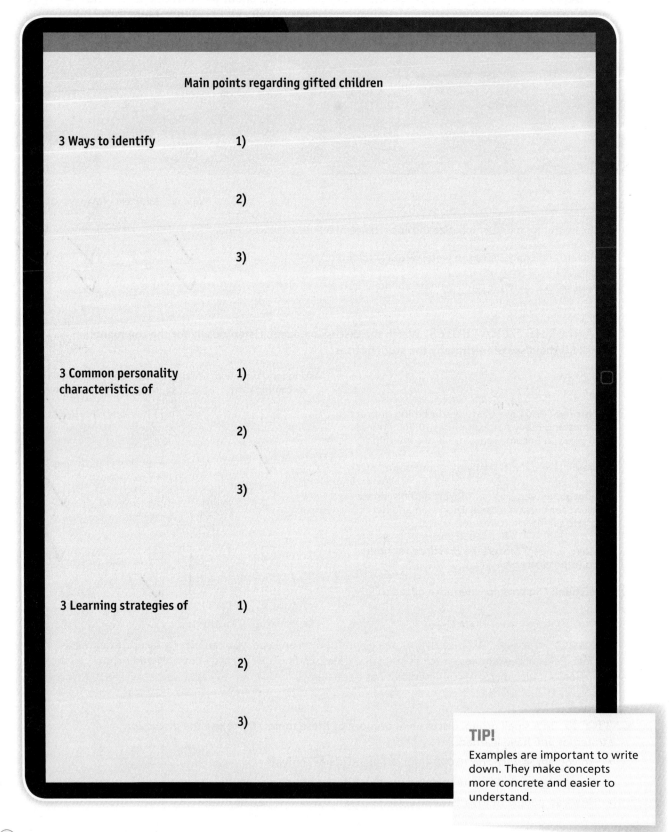

Main points regarding gifted children

3 Ways to identify

1)

2)

3)

3 Common personality characteristics of

1)

2)

3)

3 Learning strategies of

1)

2)

3)

TIP!
Examples are important to write down. They make concepts more concrete and easier to understand.

 Now you are ready to take the Unit Test and the Proficiency Assessment.

EXPRESS your ideas

Brilliant Minds

This unit has focused on gifted children, how they are identified, their personality characteristics, and how they approach learning. What aspect of giftedness is most interesting to you?

TASK **Research and give a short presentation on giftedness. Consider your audience as you prepare.**

Prepare

1 Choose one of these topics:

> Choose a gifted individual from history or a current child prodigy. Describe what is special about him or her and include any details of the person's childhood.
>
> Think of a gifted or very talented person you've known. Talk about how his or her special ability impacted you.

2 As you prepare, consider your audience.

Practice

3 Practice your presentation with a partner. Listen to your partner. Try to identify how your partner has or has not considered the audience. Ask questions.

Present

4 Work in groups of 3 or 4. Deliver your presentation to the group. At the end, ask if anyone has any questions or comments.

5 Listen to other group members' presentations. As you listen to each presentation, write down a question you would like to ask the presenter. At the end of each presentation, ask your question.

Evaluate

6 Use the *Unit 2 Presentation Evaluation Form* (in Appendix C) to think about how well your group members considered their audience.

7 For each presentation, discuss your feedback with the presenter.

Research and Presentation Strategies: Considering your audience

In order to give effective presentations, it is important to think carefully about your audience during the preparation stage. By tailoring your presentation to your audience, you can make it more accessible and engaging. Accessible and engaging presentations are more effective and have greater impact on the audience. Noting a few key principles can help you think about your audience when you prepare a presentation:

- **Organize your ideas as logically as possible.** A presentation that is coherent and has a logical flow to it is easier to understand.

- **Explain the structure of your presentation.** This will give your audience an organizational "map" and help them to follow your presentation.

- **Understand your audience's knowledge and expectations.** Identify any key terms and ideas that will need explanation, and list three things your audience is likely to want to know about the topic. Use these as a main focus as you plan your presentation.

- **Decide how interactive you want your presentation to be.** For an interactive presentation, prepare questions or statements such as:

  Please, feel free to ask questions as we go along.

  Please, hold your questions and comments until the end.

  Has anyone ever met a gifted person?

  Does anyone know who this is?

  Are there any questions or comments about this point?

3 Online Communities

CONNECT to the topic

Online communities have revolutionized the lives of millions of people. These are communities in which members interact primarily by using the Internet. For many people, online communities serve many purposes. They present the members with opportunities to communicate with like-minded people, chat with family members, express their views on topics that are meaningful to them, access rich sources of information, collaborate with people across the globe, play games, and move through virtual worlds. Online communities will be an important part of our personal and professional lives in the years to come.

A THINK ABOUT IT Take this survey about online communities. Check (√) your responses and think of reasons or examples to support them. Then compare with a partner.

	Agree	Disagree
• People can strengthen friendships by communicating online.	☐	☐
• We can learn a great deal by joining an online community.	☐	☐
• Online communication is better than face-to-face communication.	☐	☐
• Playing online games is a good use of time.	☐	☐
• Joining a professional online community can help my career.	☐	☐

B TUNE IN Listen to a conversation with entrepreneur and author Michael Petchko, talking about online communities. Then write brief answers to the questions, based on the conversation. Compare answers with a partner.

1 What short phrase summarizes what the conversation is about? _____

2 What does Petchko mean when he says "life is parallel"? _____

3 According to Petchko, how can people make a great profile? _____

4 What are two ways to communicate with others that are mentioned in the conversation?

_____

5 What is Petchko's opinion about being positive online? _____

6 Why does Petchko mention the Instagram hashtags? _____

C DISCUSS With a partner or in a small group, discuss ideas about how to create a strong online following. List at least three ideas. Then share with the class.

LEARNING OUTCOMES
In this unit, you will:
- define key terms listed in a short talk
- fact-check statements about a sociology lecture
- complete detailed statements about a sociology lecture
- identify and practice thought groups
- recognize and practice keeping a discussion on topic
- discuss the lecture with a partner to prepare for the unit test
- practice and give a presentation on Internet groups

BUILD your vocabulary

A LISTEN The boldfaced words are from the unit lecture on online communities. Listen and complete the definitions.

1 **access:** *Access* means to ___obtain___ or ___retraive___ data.

2 **business capital:** *Business capital* is goods or money that is used to ___produce___ other ___good___ or create ___income___.

3 **contribute:** *Contribute* means to give something such as money or time to help a ___person___, ___cause___, or ___orgnaization___

4 **generate:** *Generate* means to ___call___ something to ~~exist~~ exist or ___Happen___

5 **indicate:** *Indicate* means to show that ~~exast~~ exist or is ___true___.

6 **influence:** *Influence* means that a person or thing ___effect___ or ___Somthing___ in an important way.

7 **investment:** *Investment* is the money that is ___spend___ to ___create___ a ___profit___.

8 **obtain:** *Obtain* means to get something, usually after ___Makin effort___ _____.

9 **potential:** *Potential* means that there is a ___possonlity___ that something will ___Happen___ or ~~exist~~ in the future.

10 **robust:** Something that is *robust* is ___strongly formed___ or ___Made___.

B **TRY IT** Study the words and definitions with a partner, and then test your partner.

EXAMPLE

A: *What does* contribute *mean?*

B: Contribute *means that you give something such as money to help a person or an organization.*

Now take five words each and use them in simple sentences—one word per sentence. Check each other's sentences, and then copy them so that you both have a complete set of ten.

C **PAIR WORK** Cover Column A as your partner reads sentences 1–5. Listen and write the missing words in Column B. Switch roles for sentences 6–10.

COLUMN A	COLUMN B
1 All aspects of our lives are **influenced by** the people in our social networks.	1 All aspects of our lives are **influenced** _by_ the people in our social networks.
2 People have an intense **need for** social interaction.	2 People have an intense **need** _for_ social interaction.
3 Social networking gives us a place to **keep up-to-date with** one another.	3 Social networking gives us a place to **keep up-to-date** _with_ one another.
4 The success of online crowdfunding reflects **the power of** social networking.	4 The success of online crowdfunding reflects **the power** _of_ social networking.
5 If you're **involved in** business, you're probably exchanging information.	5 If you're **involved** _in_ business, you're probably exchanging information.
6 Many companies **aim to** develop an online marketplace.	6 Many companies **aim** _to_ develop an online marketplace.
7 Investment is **vital for** any business organization.	7 Investment is **vital** _for_ any business organization.
8 Members of the community are **encouraged to** participate.	8 Members of the community are **encouraged** _to_ participate.
9 These organizations are **supported by** passionate online communities.	9 These organizations are **supported** _by_ passionate online communities.
10 Players can **interact with** a number of games.	10 Players can **interact** _with_ a number of games.

FOCUS your attention

Key Terms and Definitions

In lectures, speakers often define key terms that might be new to students or those that have a special meaning.

DEFINING KEY TERMS

When lecturers focus on a key term, they often give one of these cues:

- repeat it
- spell it
- pause
- slow down
- speak more loudly
- confirm that the term was understood

- use an introductory phrase:
  There is (one key concept) ...
  One (example) is ...
  The first (theory) is ...
  Let's look at (this idea of) ...

Sometimes, a key term is followed by its definition, with a verb or phrase connecting the two. Other times, the definition precedes the key term, with a verb or phrase in between.

KEY TERM + DEFINITION

A social community is a network of friends, colleagues, and other personal contacts.
Being in a social community means you'll ...
A social community, which is a network ...

DEFINITION + KEY TERM

The location where buyers and sellers interact, which is called the marketplace, is ...
A place where the forces of supply and demand operate, referred to as the marketplace, is ...
Individuals and businesses interact as they buy and sell. That's what's known as the marketplace.

When noting definitions, it can be helpful to write the key term in capital letters and the definition beside or underneath it. For example:

CAMARADERIE = a feeling of friendship among people in a group, e.g.: The teammates developed camaraderie.

A TRY IT Listen to an excerpt from a lecture on social communication. Write the definitions for the terms.

Term	Definition
SOCIAL RECIPROCITY –	
JOINT ATTENTION –	
SELF-EXPRESSION	
SPEECH –	
FORMULATION –	
PRAGMATIC LANGUAGE –	

B PAIR WORK Compare definitions with a partner.

WATCH the lecture

A THINK ABOUT IT You are about to watch the unit lecture on the benefits of online communities. The lecturer uses these terms: *social network, personal relationships, professional connections, emotional support, entrepreneurs, leisure time,* and *sense of belonging*. Think of two sentences she might say, using some of these words.

Professor Nancy Lee

- Social

  _____

  _____

- _____

  _____

B LISTEN FOR MAIN IDEAS Close your book. Watch the lecture and take notes.

C CHECK YOUR UNDERSTANDING Use your notes. Decide if the statements are *T* (true) or *F* (false), based on the lecture. Correct any false statements.

T **1** The people in our social networks influence all aspects of our lives.

F **2** The lecturer describes six benefits of online communities.

T **3** Most people feel that they have benefited socially from being a member of a social network.

T **4** Many businesspeople are trying to expand their social networks by participating in professional online communities.

F **5** Most companies avoid trying to build online social communities.

F **6** In this lecture, *investment* refers only to monetary investment in a company.

F **7** Members of online gaming communities rarely feel that they are part of a real community.

T **8** The lecturer concludes that the Internet is useful for building social communities, but it cannot replace face-to-face interaction.

D LISTEN FOR DETAILS Close your book. Watch the lecture again. Add details to your notes and correct any mistakes.

E CHECK YOUR UNDERSTANDING Use your notes. Complete the sentences, based on the lecture.

business capital	keep up-to-date	sense of well-being
daily basis	more connected	social interaction
Internet marketing	product	venture

1 People have an intense need for _____; thus, communicating with others online is very popular.

2 Social networking allows people to _____ with one another.

3 Over 50 percent of older users report an improved _____ as a result of online social interaction.

4 Many businesspeople want to feel _____ with others in their profession.

5 SMM is a type of _____ that uses social networking websites.

6 Shared content is a type of _____.

7 Crowdfunding involves presenting a _____ or _____ to an online community.

8 Twenty-five percent of Internet users visit online gaming sites on a _____.

HEAR the language

Thought Groups

There is a trick to keeping up with fast speech: Learn to listen for "**thought groups.**" Thought groups are unified segments of speech. A speaker speaks in a short burst—a thought group—and then pauses, and then produces another thought group.

> **EXAMPLE**
> Notice these thought groups, marked with slashes (/):
> *Our focus today / is a topic in sociology / that has increasing importance for all of us / and that is online social communities /*

A LISTEN Listen to the statements from the lecture. Make a slash (/) for each pause. Note that punctuation indicating a pause has been removed.

1 As human beings we spend our entire lives growing up and learning how to live within social communities

2 Today I'd like to focus primarily on the benefits or advantages of online communities rather than on the drawbacks or disadvantages

3 We all know that one positive aspect of social networking is that it allows us to make new friends and strengthen our current relationships with old friends and family members

4 About 65 percent of college students report that they make new friends easily through social networking sites

5 A second area where online communities show consistent positive benefits concerns professional connections

6 In virtually every professional field from education to law to running a restaurant people are looking to strengthen and expand their networks

7 Often people access these networks just because they want to feel more connected with other professionals

8 Many companies aim to develop an online marketplace where they can sell their goods and services but a lot of companies also want to build a social community

9 Nonprofit organizations like the Red Cross the World Wildlife Fund or TED all need social communities to raise awareness of their ideas and causes and also to raise funds for operations

10 A recent poll in *Game Studies* a journal of computer game research suggests that approximately one out of every four Internet users visits online gaming sites on a daily basis

B PAIR WORK Practice saying the sentences with a partner. Focus on pausing between thought groups.

TALK about the topic

Keeping a Discussion on Topic

🔊 ▶️ **A FOLLOW THE DISCUSSION** Watch as the students talk about social networking. Then read each repetition or paraphrase and check (√) who said it.

Kenzie   Hugh   Shelley   Ben

	Kenzie	Hugh	Shelley	Ben
1 "So you think there are some downsides to social networking?"	☐	☐	☐	☐
2 "Yeah, nothing is perfect."	☐	☐	☐	☐
3 "So about a third of the campaigns have been successful?"	☐	☐	☐	☐
4 "Oh, so she became popular first and then raised money second."	☐	☐	☐	☐
5 "All right, so we have examples of successful film and music campaigns."	☐	☐	☐	☐

🔊 ▶️ **B LEARN THE STRATEGIES** Watch the discussion again. Listen closely for the comments. Check (√) the discussion strategy the student uses. More than one answer may be possible.

	Asking for opinions or ideas	Expressing an opinion	Keeping a discussion on topic
1 **Ben:** "Well, first, I wonder if the lecture was a little bit too positive."	☐	☐	☐
2 **Kenzie:** "Let's focus on the lecture."	☐	☐	☐
3 **Kenzie:** "So does anyone have any examples of successful crowdfunding campaigns?"	☐	☐	☐
4 **Shelley:** "Do you know of any successful music projects?"	☐	☐	☐

Discussion Strategy While tangents (related topics) can be interesting during a conversation, it's fair to remind others of the focus. Common expressions for **keeping a discussion on topic** include *That's interesting, but let's focus on ... ; I'd like to get back to ... ; We're getting a little off track ... ;* and the very informal *Anyway!* The next step—listening to the comments once the conversation is refocused—is where your learning begins!

C TRY IT In a small group, discuss one or more of these topics. Try to use the discussion strategies you have learned.

• Ben thinks that the lecturer was too positive about social networking. Do you agree?

• Shelley says that almost one-third of the crowdfunding campaigns on Kickstarter are successful. What do you think are the good and bad points of crowdfunding?

• Would you be interested in participating in a crowdfunding project? Why or why not? If yes, what type of project would you be interested in?

REVIEW your notes

REVIEW With a partner, review your notes from the lecture. What key terms have you identified? Have you written any definitions? Take turns defining the key terms from the lecture. Use the key terms and definitions to reconstruct the main points of the lecture.

Definitions

Social networking –

Professional networking site –

Social Media Marketing (SMM) –

Shared content –

Crowdfunding –

Online gaming community –

TIP!
Be sure to write down key terms. You can always look up a definition later if you missed it in class or the meaning wasn't clear.

 Now you are ready to take the Unit Test and the Proficiency Assessment.

EXPRESS your ideas

Cyber Groups

This unit has focused on the benefits of online communities. What are your own ideas about or personal experiences with online communities?

TASK Research and give a short presentation on social networking. Apply the practice techniques as you prepare.

Prepare

1 Choose one of these topics:

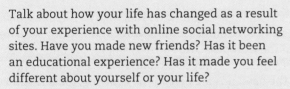

> Talk about how your life has changed as a result of your experience with online social networking sites. Have you made new friends? Has it been an educational experience? Has it made you feel different about yourself or your life?
>
> *Either* read two articles *or* listen to two online audio / video clips that discuss the benefits or problems associated with social networking sites. Identify information that does not appear in the lecture for this unit and decide which information you found most interesting.
>
> Interview at least five students about one aspect of online communities. For instance, you might focus on people involved in a professional site, a crowdfunding site, or a gaming site. Ask them questions—for example: *How have you benefited from being a part of the online community? Have there been any downsides? What recommendations do you have for new members?* Synthesize the ideas carefully and tell your classmates what you have discovered.

Practice

2 Practice your presentation with a partner. Listen to your partner. Notice how he or she uses the practice techniques. Ask two questions to get more details about the topic.

3 As you practice, try to apply the strategies for practicing.

Present

4 Work in groups of 3 or 4. Deliver your presentation to the group. At the end, ask if anyone has any questions or comments.

5 Listen to your group members' presentations.

Evaluate

6 Use the *Unit 3 Presentation Evaluation Form* (in Appendix C) to think about how well your group members prepared for their presentations.

7 For each presentation, discuss your feedback with the presenter.

Research and Presentation Strategies: Practicing

Practicing will help you to become more familiar with the ideas you wish to communicate, the organization of those ideas, and how you wish to communicate them. Here are some issues to consider:

- **Create authentic conditions.** Practice your presentation in an authentic way. For example, if you will stand when presenting, then stand when you practice. If you will use slides or video in your presentation, then use them when you practice.

- **Get in the right mindset.** There is a saying that *practice makes perfect*. This means that when you practice, you should do it with good effort and concentration.

- **Use peers as a sounding board.** Ask some classmates to watch you practice and to give you feedback about all aspects of it, such as the ideas, organization, word choice, eye contact, gestures, and voice.

- **Record yourself.** Recording yourself will allow you to hear how you sound. The recording can let you know more about your strengths and weaknesses as a presenter.

- **Experiment with different approaches.** After getting feedback, try to change and improve your presentation by trying different approaches to what you are saying and how you say it.

- **Depart from the script.** While planning what you want to say is important, do not follow a script too closely. You want to give a presentation that feels fresh and spontaneous. The audience wants to hear *you*, not a memorized speech.

4   Core Business Skills

CONNECT to the topic

Our rapidly internationalizing world is causing dramatic changes in the ways that many companies operate. The ease with which we can travel to far-away places and communicate almost instantaneously with anyone with a device connected to the Internet has reshaped the workplace. As a result, employees must develop new skills, new types of knowledge, and new ways of thinking if they are to make contributions to their company and enhance its competitiveness. Because the demands are constantly evolving, modern employees must be life-long learners who are flexible and ready to acquire new skills and forms of knowledge.

A THINK ABOUT IT List at least five skills or types of knowledge that you believe are important in today's business world. Then discuss three of your ideas with a partner.

- _____
- _____
- _____
- _____
- _____

B TUNE IN Listen to an interview with business consultant Melissa Kramer, who talks about the advantages of a diverse workforce. Then decide if the statements are *True* or *False*, based on the interview. Compare answers with a partner. Explain what's untrue about the false statements.

	True	False
1 The major categories of diversity include age, race, and religion.		✓
2 One part of managing diversity involves minimizing its disadvantages.	✓	
3 One advantage of a diverse workforce is that employees are more motivated.	✓	
4 Kramer implies that access to overseas markets is a goal of many companies.	✓	
5 According to Kramer, one disadvantage is that a diverse workforce can generate a confusing number of different ideas.		✓
6 Kramer feels positively about employees who have diverse points of view.	✓	

C PAIR WORK Do you think that companies should make an effort to hire a diverse workforce? Why or why not? List five reasons to support your view. Then discuss with a partner.

LEARNING OUTCOMES
In this unit, you will:
- practice using symbols and abbreviations in your notes
- articulate the main ideas of a business lecture
- fact-check statements about a business lecture
- identify and practice sounds that influence the pronunciation of -s
- recognize and practice bringing a discussion to a close
- organize and add notations to your lecture notes to prepare for the unit test
- give an organized presentation about your experience with a core business skill

BUILD your vocabulary

A LISTEN The boldfaced words are from the unit lecture on core business skills. Listen to each sentence. Then guess the meaning of the boldfaced word. Work with a partner.

1 It is important that employees gradually **acquire** more skills as they work. Adding to their skill set allows them to work more effectively.

2 International projects require **collaboration** among diverse people. Working with people from different countries can be both challenging and rewarding.

3 Learning to use many types of computer software can be a **daunting** task, but learning to use one type can help us learn another. In this way, the task becomes more manageable.

4 A **diverse** workforce can improve the decision-making process. By including various individuals, managers can gather more information and make better decisions.

5 When employees work together **harmoniously**, rather than wasting time arguing and disagreeing, they can make faster progress.

6 Researchers say that there are many kinds of **intelligence**. For example, interpersonal intelligence is the ability to understand and interact effectively with other people.

7 Companies must **navigate** a rapidly changing business environment. Important decisions affecting the direction of the company must be made nearly every day.

8 Every **occupation** involves human interaction, so communication skills are important. For instance, people in management positions must constantly interact with others.

9 Because many professionals must read and listen to large amounts of information, they must learn to identify key points and **prioritize** the information.

10 New **technologies** have completely changed how people communicate. Computers and other devices such as cell phones and tablets allow people to exchange information across vast distances almost instantly.

B TRY IT Choose the best definition for each boldfaced word.

1 acquire advanced skills
  a lose
  b repeatedly use
  c work to gain ⭕

2 the company encourages **collaboration**
  a working in the same field
  b competing against one another
  c working together ⭕

3 a **daunting** task
  a simple
  b interesting
  c difficult ⭕

4 diverse reasons
  a very important
  b a variety of different ⭕
  c logical

5 working **harmoniously** together
  a in sync ⭕
  b indifferently
  c anxiously

6 high level of **intelligence**
  a aptitude ⭕
  b industriousness
  c persistence

7 navigate the website
  a make a surprising discovery about
  b find one's way around ⭕
  c create

8 changing his **occupation**
  a opinion
  b job ⭕
  c approach

9 prioritize information
  a increase the amount of
  b rank ⭕
  c replace ❌

10 useful **technologies**
  a machines created using knowledge ⭕
  b people
  c strategies

C PAIR WORK Cover Group A as your partner reads sentences 1–5. Listen and write the missing words in Group B. Your partner corrects your answers. Switch roles for 6–10.

GROUP A

1 Communication skills are about **connecting with** people.

2 Social intelligence is **related to** your intuition.

3 Social intelligence is a term **coined by** Edward Thorndike.

4 Collaboration means **getting along with** diverse groups of people.

5 We must develop **sensitivity to** different people.

6 The effectiveness of the workforce **depends on** the social intelligence of the people involved.

7 It's impossible to **take in** all the new information.

8 We have to be able to ask good questions to **find out** what we need to know.

9 You ask questions and you **try out** the new skills.

10 Using this strategy **moves us into** a positive learning cycle.

GROUP B

1 Communication skills are about **connecting** with people.

2 Social intelligence is **related** to your intuition.

3 Social intelligence is a term **coined** by Edward Thorndike.

4 Collaboration means **getting along** with diverse groups of people.

5 We must develop **sensitivity** to different people.

6 The effectiveness of the workforce **depends** on the social intelligence of the people involved.

7 It's impossible to **take** in all the new information.

8 We have to be able to ask good questions to **find** out what we need to know.

9 You ask questions and you **try** out the new skills.

10 Using this strategy **moves us** into a positive learning cycle.

FOCUS your attention

Symbols and Abbreviations

Listening to a lecture can be very challenging. One useful strategy that can help you is to use symbols and abbreviations. This speeds up your note-taking and helps you to keep up with the lecturer. You will often use your notes several weeks after you originally took them, so make sure all of your symbols and abbreviations are clear and easy to understand.

=	equals; is the same as	[	includes
≠	does not equal / is not the same as	]	excludes
		+ or &	and; also
>	is more than / larger than	...	continues; and so on
<	is less than / smaller than	$	dollars
∴	therefore; as a result / because	%	percent
		#	number
↑	to increase	~	for example or approximately
↓	to decrease		
→	leads to; causes	Δ	change
←	is caused by; depends on	k	thousand

ad	advertisement	fb	feedback
av	average	glob	globalization
co	company	intl	international
cult diff	cultural difference	Prof JY	Professor Julian Young
def	definition		
ex or e.g.	example		

A TRY IT Listen to an excerpt from a report on job trends. Take notes and use symbols and abbreviations.

B PAIR WORK Compare notes with a partner. Did you use similar symbols and abbreviations?

WATCH the lecture

A THINK ABOUT IT You are about to watch the unit lecture on core business skills. What skills do you think are important in today's workplace?

_____

_____

Professor Julian Young

B LISTEN FOR MAIN IDEAS Close your book. Watch the lecture and take notes.

C CHECK YOUR UNDERSTANDING Use your notes. Complete the mains ideas, based on the lecture.

connecting	machine interfacing
emotional states	sense-making
growth sector	social intelligence
hands-on experience	strategy
information	technical in nature

1 The core set of business skills applies to _____ professions.

2 Communications, the first skill set, concerns _____ with people, not just communicating information.

3 The second skill set, _____ , is basically the ability to understand the _____ of people.

4 The third skill set, which is a bit _____ , is called _____ .

5 The fourth skill set is _____ . This skill set requires us to make sense of the _____ around us.

6 All four skill sets can be acquired through _____ .

7 A strong desire to learn is the most important _____ to use.

D LISTEN FOR DETAILS Close your book. Watch the lecture again. Add details to your notes and correct any mistakes.

E CHECK YOUR UNDERSTANDING Use your notes. Decide if the statements are *T* (true) or *F* (false), based on the lecture. Correct any false statements.

_____ **1** Asking questions is one example of good communication skills.

_____ **2** The term *social intelligence* was coined by Edward Thorndike in the 1930s.

_____ **3** It is important to develop sensitivity to different ways of viewing the world.

_____ **4** Two examples of computer technologies mentioned in the lecture are video chats and cloud computing.

_____ **5** It is often best to depend on IT professionals when dealing with technology.

_____ **6** Sense-making can involve categorizing information.

_____ **7** The positive learning cycle entails setting goals, performing, and evaluating.

HEAR the language

Sounds Influencing -s

When English is spoken quickly, one **sound** can take on the characteristics of the sound next to it. One such change occurs when a preceding sound affects a following sound. One common example of this occurs in plural nouns in English. For example, the /g/ sound in *bag* causes the plural -s to be pronounced as /z/ (*bags*). In contrast, the /k/ sound in *pack* causes the plural -s to be pronounced as /s/ (*packs*).

EXAMPLES

Notice how the sounds before the -s in the underlined words influence the pronunciation:

/s/   *We've got four skill se**ts** to review.*

/z/   *Last time, we looked at tren**ds** in the job market.*

/əz/   *There are many advanta**ges** to being bilingual.*

A LISTEN Listen and complete the statements from the lecture. Notice how the plural nouns are pronounced.

1 Of course, good _____ must be able to express themselves clearly and positively—in both speaking and writing.

2 Good communication _____ means you can give and understand _____ , listen to _____ and learn new _____ , make _____ , ask _____ , and give convincing _____ when someone asks you a question.

3 And nowadays that means getting along with diverse _____ of people.

4 Just having email _____ and web _____ with the people on your project team isn't enough.

5 In the same way that we communicate fluently with our business _____ in personal _____ , we also need to navigate fluently in different _____ and software.

6 We need to be able to create and manage _____ and _____ and _____ .

7 We need to be able to draw reasonable _____ based on what we understand.

8 Well, the good news is that all of these _____ can be learned through _____ experience.

B PAIR WORK Practice saying the sentences with a partner. Focus on pronouncing the -s endings correctly.

TALK about the topic

Bringing a Discussion to a Close

A FOLLOW THE DISCUSSION Watch as the students talk about social intelligence. Then read each question and check (√) who answers it.

Hugh   Shelley   Ben   Kenzie

	Hugh	Shelley	Ben	Kenzie
1 "Do you think this sort of skill, this sort of social intelligence, can be learned? Or do people have it naturally?"	☐	☐	☐	☐
2 "Bias. Am I saying that right?"	☐	☐	☐	☐
3 "We talk with people from five or ten different countries every day at school, right?"	☐	☐	☐	☐
4 "I wonder how well we can empathize with someone from another culture?"	☐	☐	☐	☐

B LEARN THE STRATEGIES Watch the discussion again. Listen closely for the comments. Check (√) the discussion strategy the student uses.

	Bringing a discussion to a close	Expressing an opinion	Offering a fact or example
1 **Shelley:** "For example, there are social intelligence training courses online."	☐	☐	☐
2 **Ben:** "I think those courses basically teach people to be, you know, more aware of themselves and others."	☐	☐	☐
3 **Kenzie:** "I mean, look at us, for instance."	☐	☐	☐
4 **Kenzie:** "I think empathy is also a big part of it."	☐	☐	☐
5 **Hugh:** "So, we've talked a lot about interesting things that we can develop further. Why don't we sign off for now?"	☐	☐	☐

Discussion Strategy In study groups or other organized conversations, it is eventually necessary to **bring the discussion to a close**. The following expressions can be used to end a discussion: *OK, I think we're finished ... ; So thanks everyone. This was a good meeting ... ;* and *I think we've covered all of the points ... .*

C TRY IT In a small group, discuss one or more of these topics. Try to use the discussion strategies you have learned.

- How would you define social intelligence? What are the characteristics of a person with a high level of social intelligence?
- Do you think that social intelligence is important in most workplaces? Why or why not?
- Do you think that it's possible for a person to develop social intelligence? If so, how can it be done?

REVIEW your notes

REVIEW With a partner, review your notes from the lecture. Do they include any symbols or abbreviations? If so, do you remember what they mean? Reconstruct the lecture by completing the outline below, using symbols and abbreviations where appropriate. Then deliver the lecture to a classmate.

> ### Core Business Skills
>
> Skill set 1 =
>
> 5 examples of good comm. skills
> 1
> 2
> 3
> 4
> 5
>
> Skill set 2 =
> Social intell. def. =
> Ex. of diversity:
>
> Skill set 3 =
> Examples:
>
> Skill set 4 =
> Sense-making def. =
> Examples:
>
> How to acquire the skill sets
> 1
> 2
> 3
> 4
> 5

🔊 **Now you are ready to take the Unit Test and the Proficiency Assessment.**

EXPRESS your ideas

Knowledge, Skills, and Abilities

This unit has focused on core business skills in the modern world. Which skill seems most essential, in your view? Which is your greatest strength? Your greatest weakness?

TASK Research and give a short presentation on your experience with a core business skill. Develop your presentation in a way that will make the organization of your presentation clear to your audience.

Prepare

1 Choose one of these topics:

Describe someone you know who you believe has a high level of social intelligence. Give examples of how the person demonstrates social intelligence.

Talk about your experiences communicating successfully with people from other cultures. What "guidelines" for successful communication can you recommend to others?

Talk about some of your knowledge of machine interfacing by explaining how to use one piece of software. Explain the benefits of being able to use that software.

Practice

2 Practice your presentation with a partner. Listen to your partner. As you listen, notice how effective the presentation's organization is. Make 2 suggestions for how your partner might improve the organization.

Present

3 Work in groups of 3 or 4. Deliver your presentation to the group. At the end, ask if anyone has any questions or comments.

4 Listen to other group members' presentations.

Evaluate

5 Use the *Unit 4 Presentation Evaluation Form* (in Appendix C) to think about how clear your group members made the organization of their presentations.

6 For each presentation, discuss your feedback with the presenter.

Research and Presentation Strategies: Giving an organized presentation

For any presentation to be successful, it is essential that it be organized. Here are five strategies to help you make the organization of your presentation clear to your audience:

- **Preview the main ideas in the beginning of your presentation.** In the introduction of your presentation, tell the audience the main points you will talk about. You can do this using a phrase such as *Today I will talk about three issues regarding ... .*

- **Develop one main idea in each paragraph.** You can think of your presentation as having several main ideas, with each idea developed into a paragraph. Each paragraph should be about only one topic, and the sentences in each paragraph should connect to one another in a clear, logical way.

- **Clearly indicate when you change topics.** Tell the audience when you are changing topics by using phrases such as *The second important point concerns ...* and *The third and final reason is ... .*

- **Highlight the key points in your presentation.** Clearly tell the audience what the main points are by using phrases such as *The most important reason is ... ; We must remember that ... ;* and *One key idea concerns ... .*

- **Review and summarize the main ideas at the end of your presentation.** When you conclude your presentation, restate your main points. It is a good idea to paraphrase what you said at the beginning of the presentation.

5 Memory

CONNECT to the topic

In many ways, we are our memories. When we think about who we are, we think about the events we've experienced, the people we've known, the places where we've lived and visited, as well as our ideas and feelings about a great many things. All of this is stored in our memory system. The mysteries of human memory have intrigued people for thousands of years. However, only in the past few decades have researchers begun to understand why some moments in our lives become etched in our memories forever while others evaporate almost immediately.

A THINK ABOUT IT Take this survey about memory. Check (✓) your responses and think of reasons or examples to support them. Then compare with a partner.

	Never	Sometimes	Usually	Always
• I can easily remember what I did yesterday.				✓
• I can easily remember conversations I had a month ago.		✓		
• I can easily recall the faces of people I met years ago.		✓		
• I can remember something better if I talk about it.				✓
• I can remember things that I'm interested in.				✓
• I can remember something if I've read it several times.				✓

B TUNE IN Listen to an interview with memory competitor Sarah MacNamara, who discusses a technique to improve memory. Then decide if the statements are *True* or *False*, based on the interview. Compare answers with a partner. Explain what's untrue about the false statements.

	True	False
1 MacNamara talks about one memory secret.		
2 MacNamara believes that repetition is the key to a good memory.		
3 In this case, *enhanced* means that information is repeated several times.		
4 MacNamara says that storytelling is a creative act.		
5 According to MacNamara, fictional stories are uninteresting.		
6 MacNamara's ideas fundamentally concern personalizing information.		

C PAIR WORK Do you think that the enhanced storytelling technique could be effective? Why or why not? List three reasons to support your view. Then discuss with a partner.

LEARNING OUTCOMES
In this unit, you will:

- listen for language that signals cause-and-effect relationships
- recognize the main points of a cognitive psychology lecture
- extract details from a cognitive psychology lecture
- identify and practice sounds that influence the pronunciation of -t
- recognize and practice getting a discussion started
- review and summarize your lecture notes to prepare for the unit test
- connect with your audience while presenting on enhancing memory

BUILD your vocabulary

A LISTEN The boldfaced words are from the unit lecture on memory. Listen to each sentence. Then guess the meaning of the boldfaced word. Work with a partner.

1 **Brain chemicals** can make people feel very excited or very sad. These natural substances have an extremely strong influence on our feelings.

2 Many of our memories, such as the facts and ideas that we learn in school, are **conscious**. We can recall them and explain them to others.

3 In the past **decade**, researchers have learned many new things about how memory works. And even more progress is expected in the next ten years.

4 Some of our knowledge about how to do things, such as riding a bicycle, is mostly **implicit**. We can ride the bicycle, but it's very difficult to tell another person how to do it.

5 We often think about **logical** relationships when studying something. For instance, what is the reasonable cause of something, or what will be the likely result of some event?

6 When we do mathematics, we **manipulate** information in one part of our memory system by adding, subtracting, or changing the numbers.

7 Some **psychologists** have studied the types of memory we have and how to improve memory. Thanks to this specialized study of the mind, we now know much more about memory than we did a generation ago.

8 When we feel strong emotions, our brains **release** substances. These substances go to specific parts of our brain and help us remember that event.

9 The most important function of our memory system is that it can **retain** information for long periods of time. Because of this, we can remember events that happened many years ago.

10 Some memories are stored only **temporarily**. They can be recalled very briefly, and then they fade away.

B TRY IT Match each word to the correct definition.

_f_ 1 handle, control, or move something

_d_ 2 understood, but not stated directly

_b_ 3 something we notice or are aware of

_e_ 4 reasonable and sensible

_i_ 5 keep facts in your memory

_a_ 6 substances that influence our thoughts and emotions

_j_ 7 for a short time

_g_ 8 people who study how the mind works

_h_ 9 let something go

_c_ 10 ten years

a brain chemicals

b conscious

c decade

d implicit

e logical

f manipulate

g psychologists

h release

i retain

j temporarily

Now say each word to yourself. Write *N* if it is a noun, *V* if it is a verb, *A* if it is an adjective, and *AV* if it is an adverb. Then use the word in a sentence.

____ 1 brain chemicals   ____ 5 logical   ____ 8 release

____ 2 conscious   ____ 6 manipulate   ____ 9 retain

____ 3 decade   ____ 7 psychologists   ____ 10 temporarily

____ 4 implicit

C PAIR WORK With a partner, take turns completing each sentence with the correct form of the word. Notice the boldfaced words. Read the completed sentences aloud. Review any words you don't understand.

conscious	consciously	consciousness

1 Some of the information in our memory is _consciously_ **available to** us.

2 Some memory enhancement techniques are **concerned with** making a _consciousness_ effort to relate ideas to one another.

imply	implicit	implicitly

3 Mika _implicitly_ **agreed with** Jonas by smiling at him and nodding her head.

4 The fact that information in our mind can be **stored for** different amounts of time **seems to** _imply_ that we have different memory systems.

logic	logical	logically

5 Our memory system is absolutely **crucial for** _logical_ thought.

6 Understanding **relationships between** ideas requires **the use of** _logic_.

manipulate	manipulative	manipulation

7 When we _manipulate_ ideas in our minds, we can sometimes **come up with** new ways of thinking about issues.

8 Jessie's _manipulation_ of the information allowed him to remember it longer.

FOCUS your attention

Cause-and-Effect Relationships

Academic lectures often include information about cause-and-effect relationships. These relationships are very important because they clarify how different aspects of a topic relate to one another. Understanding cause-and-effect relationships will help you remember the information in the lecture.

SOME WAYS LECTURERS MIGHT EXPRESS A CAUSE-AND-EFFECT RELATIONSHIP

*If you hear something, **then** your auditory memory will be activated.*

*You remember this theory **because** we talked about it for almost an hour.*

***Because of** his research, our understanding of memory is clearer.*

*Using more senses **causes** us to remember more.*

*Emotion **affects** how well we remember events.*

***The effect of** repeating information is better recall.*

*Better memory **results in** more learning.*

A TRY IT Listen to an excerpt from a lecture on caffeine and memory. What phrases do you hear that express a cause-and-effect relationship? Note below what causes and effects the speaker mentions.

cause → effect

B PAIR WORK Compare notes with a partner.

WATCH the lecture

A THINK ABOUT IT You are about to watch the unit lecture on memory. List three strategies that you use to remember information better.

Professor Brian Murphy

- _____
  _____

- _____
  _____

- _____
  _____

B LISTEN FOR MAIN IDEAS Close your book. Watch the lecture and take notes.

C CHECK YOUR UNDERSTANDING Use your notes. Complete the main ideas, based on the lecture.

affective strategies	implicit	retain
cognitive strategies	initial moment	senses
consciously available	manipulate	store
emotional	meaningful	unconscious
hold	recall	

1 A simple definition of memory is the ability to _____ , _____ , and _____ information.

2 Sensory memory concerns the _____ that we perceive something with our _____ .

3 Working memory is where we temporarily _____ and _____ information.

4 Long-term memories are information that was initially processed in working memory in _____ and possibly _____ ways.

5 Declarative memory is all of the information that is _____ to us.

6 Procedural memories are _____ and _____ .

7 _____ are concerned with thinking in more effective ways.

8 _____ are concerned with controlling our emotional responses.

🔊 ▶️ **D LISTEN FOR DETAILS** Close your book. Watch the lecture again. Add details to your notes and correct any mistakes.

E CHECK YOUR UNDERSTANDING Use your notes. Choose the phrase that best completes each idea, based on the lecture.

1 Sensory memory lasts approximately _____ .
  a 1–5 milliseconds   **b** 10–50 milliseconds   **c** 100–500 milliseconds

2 The way to record an experience in more ways in our brain is to _____ .
  a repeat the experience   **b** talk about the experience   **c** use multiple senses

3 The type of memory that is crucial for adding numbers or understanding logical relationships is _____ .
  a sensory memory   **b** working memory   **c** long-term memory

4 Long-term memory lasts from 30 seconds to _____ .
  a several days   **b** several months   **c** your entire lifetime

5 Riding a bicycle and playing a musical instrument are examples of _____ .
  a working memory   **b** procedural memory   **c** declarative memory

6 _____ concern(s) talking about information in ways that are personally meaningful.
  a Declarative memory   **b** Verbal elaboration   **c** Affective strategies

7 Emotions affect memory formation because they cause _____ .
  a the release of brain chemicals   **b** the release of hormones   **c** the use of better affective strategies

8 A secondary benefit of using affective strategies is that they can increase a person's sense of _____ .
  a fun and challenge   **b** progress and learning   **c** variety

HEAR the language

Sounds Influencing -t

When English is spoken quickly, one sound can be **influenced** by the characteristics of the sounds next to it. This is called "assimilation." One kind of assimilation occurs when a following sound affects a preceding sound. This kind of change can occur in a single word, such as when the /t/ in the word *rating* is pronounced as /d/. Or it can occur in two adjacent words, such as when the /t/ sound in *about* becomes /d/ in the phrase *about an hour*.

EXAMPLES

Notice how each boldfaced -t is pronounced almost like /d/:

*Joan no**t**ed down much of what the teacher said in the class lectures.*

*I study three times a day for abou**t** an hour each time.*

A LISTEN Listen and complete the statements from the lecture. Write the words you hear. Notice how the *t* is pronounced in each case.

1 As _____ _____ our study of the brain's various functions, we're going to look at the topic of memory.

2 Now it sounds simple, but if you think _____ _____ , in many ways, we are our memories.

3 All of this information is stored in a _____ _____ brain systems that handle the different types of memory.

4 So first, let's look at three types of memory _____ _____ been _____ by psychologists.

5 And finally, there's what's called long-term memory, which is memory that's stored for as little as _____ seconds to as long as your entire lifetime.

6 Now, there are two subtypes of long-term memory. There's _____ memory and procedural memory.

7 All of your experiences and conscious memories fall into this _____ .

8 This type of memory can be improved if we use certain strategies, so I want to talk about two types of memory strategies _____ _____ useful in school: cognitive _____ and affective _____ .

9 That means _____ _____ you study, you should think about and verbalize information _____ .

10 See, the point of trying the affective strategy is that it will increase _____ _____ your memory, _____ _____ your sense of fun, and challenge, and interest.

B PAIR WORK Practice saying the sentences with a partner. Focus on pronouncing each influenced -t correctly.

TALK about the topic

Getting a Discussion Started

A FOLLOW THE DISCUSSION Watch as the students talk about memory. Read each question. Then check (√) who answers it.

Rob   Alana   Ayman   Molly

	Rob	Alana	Ayman	Molly
1 "So guys, does anyone think that any of these memorization strategies actually work?"	☐	☐	☐	☐
2 "What did he call it?"	☐	☐	☐	☐
3 "Well, isn't that kind of common sense?"	☐	☐	☐	☐
4 "Like, do any of you think that you can actually change your feelings about a subject?"	☐	☐	☐	☐

B LEARN THE STRATEGIES Watch the discussion again. Listen closely for the comments. Check (√) the discussion strategy the student uses.

	Getting a discussion started	Keeping a discussion on topic	Offering a fact or example
1 **Rob:** "So why don't we start by going over some of the memorization strategies."	☐	☐	☐
2 **Ayman:** "I grew up learning everything via memorization."	☐	☐	☐
3 **Rob:** "What about the affective strategy that he mentioned?"	☐	☐	☐
4 **Molly:** "We started meeting every Sunday at Café Roma to study, and we'd have questions prepared for each other and stuff."	☐	☐	☐

Discussion Strategy In study groups or other organized conversations, **getting a discussion started** on time is in everyone's best interest. While chitchat before a discussion officially starts is natural, it's important for someone to prompt the discussion to begin. Expressions for getting a discussion started include *Why don't we start by ... ; It looks like everyone's here. Ben, can you start us off?;* and *So, today we're going to discuss ... .*

C TRY IT In a small group, discuss one or more of these topics. Try to use the discussion strategies you have learned.

- Do you agree that memorization can be an effective approach to learning?
- Can you think of other ways to make a class more interesting?

REVIEW your notes

REVIEW Read your notes. With a partner, take turns explaining the ideas from the lecture, using the following headings to help you. Give examples or add comments as you discuss. Then complete these notes together.

· 3 main types of memory systems:

   1)

   2)

   3)

· Differences between declarative and procedural memory:

· Def. of cognitive strategies:

Ex.:

· Def. of affective strategies:

Ex.:

TIP!

Try to mark cause-and-effect relationships in your notes. This will help you understand how different ideas or processes are related.

 Now you are ready to take the Unit Test and the Proficiency Assessment.

EXPRESS your ideas

Brain Training

This unit has focused on memory, which is a key aspect of cognition. In what situations do you use memory? What aspect of your memory would you like to improve?

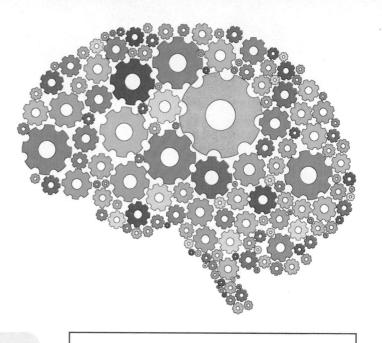

TASK Research and give a short presentation on enhancing memory. Try to connect with your audience.

Prepare

1 Choose and research one of these techniques for enhancing memory, or use your own idea:

> distributed practice
>
> expanding rehearsal
>
> the Journey System
>
> mnemonics
>
> mind maps
>
> personalization
>
> the Roman Room method

2 Try out the technique. Does it work for you?

Practice

3 Practice your presentation with a partner. Listen to your partner.

4 As you practice, try to use the strategies for connecting with your audience.

Present

5 Work in groups of 3 or 4. Deliver your presentation to the group. At the end, ask if anyone has any questions or comments.

6 Listen to other group members' presentations.

Evaluate

7 Use the *Unit 5 Presentation Evaluation Form* (in Appendix C) to think about how well your group members connected with the audience.

8 For each presentation, discuss your feedback with the presenter.

Research and Presentation Strategies: Connecting with your audience

To deliver a successful presentation, you need to connect with your audience. Here are four strategies you can use to create a positive connection:

- **Use a device, such as an interesting quotation or an interesting fact, to get the audience's attention at the beginning and at the end of your presentation.** By using devices such as these, you have a greater chance of introducing your topic in an interesting way, and concluding the presentation effectively.

- **Display confidence in what you are saying through your voice, facial expressions, and body language.** Having confidence allows you to create a positive relationship with your audience. Audience members want to listen to presenters who understand their topic well and are therefore confident speakers.

- **Be attentive to your audience by focusing your attention on them, not on your notes or slides.** Effective presenters give audience members the feeling that the presentation is a form of *personal* communication.

- **Develop rapport with your audience by referring to shared knowledge or experiences, using humor, or asking questions that encourage audience members to think about your topic actively.** A connection with the audience can occur when you make the audience feel an emotional or intellectual connection to you.

6 The Science of Love

CONNECT to the topic

Throughout recorded history, one topic has attracted generation after generation of artists, musicians, and writers: love. Even today, love is seen by many people as a mysterious, uncontrollable force that can never be fully understood. However, this is exactly what researchers in many academic fields have been trying to do over the past 40 years. While some people would say that these researchers have made great progress explaining the cognitive and emotional makeup of love, others would say that love should forever remain mysterious and inexplicable.

A THINK ABOUT IT Take this survey about love. Check (✓) your responses and think of reasons or examples to support them. Then compare with a partner.

	Agree	Disagree
• Love is the strongest emotion.	✓	
• Love is the same in all cultures.	✓	
• There are many kinds of love.	✓	
• People who are in love don't behave rationally.		
• Love develops in a predictable way.		
• Love can never be explained by science.		

B TUNE IN Listen to an interview with marriage counselor Sylvie McDonald. Then write brief answers to the questions, based on the interview.

1 What single word or phrase describes what the discussion is about? _____

2 Why are good communication skills important in a marriage? _____

3 What "goes into overdrive" when we fall in love? _____

4 What does McDonald say about "misunderstandings"? _____

5 What example does McDonald give about cultural differences in communication? _____

6 Does McDonald believe cross-cultural marriages are "worth the effort"? _____

C DISCUSS With a partner or in a small group, discuss benefits and challenges cross-cultural marriages might present. List three benefits and three challenges. Then share with the class.

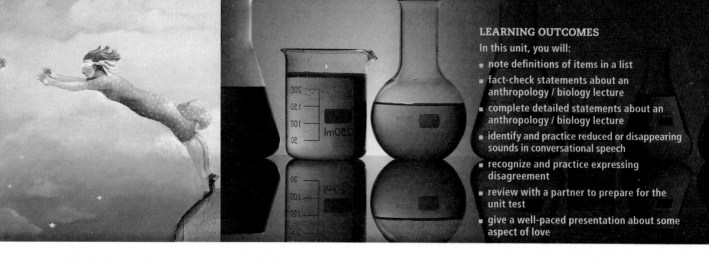

BUILD your vocabulary

A LISTEN The boldfaced words are from the unit lecture on love. Listen and complete the definitions.

1 anthropologists: Anthropologists study _____, their _____, and their _____.

2 attachment: Having an attachment to someone or something means that you feel strong _____, _____, or _____ toward that person or thing.

3 characteristic: A special _____ or _____ that someone or something has.

4 emotion: An emotion is a _____ _____ _____ such as love or hate.

5 enhance: If you enhance something, you _____ _____ _____.

6 hormone: A hormone is a substance in our body that influences our _____, _____, and _____.

7 invoke: If something invokes a feeling, it _____ that feeling to _____.

8 mutual: This is a feeling or action that is _____ or _____ by two or more people toward _____.

9 prospective: Prospective means that a person is _____ to _____ a particular thing or that the event is _____ _____.

10 romantic: Romantic people express strong feelings of _____ in their _____ and _____.

B **TRY IT** Study the words and definitions with a partner, and then test your partner.

EXAMPLE

A: *What are anthropologists?*

B: *Anthropologists study people, their societies, and their beliefs.*

Now take five words each and use them in simple sentences—one word per sentence. Check each other's sentences, and then copy them so that you both have a complete set of ten.

1 anthropologists: _____

2 attachment: _____

3 characteristic: _____

4 emotion: _____

5 enhance: _____

6 hormone: _____

7 invoke: _____

8 mutual: _____

9 prospective: _____

10 romantic: _____

C **PAIR WORK** With a partner, reorder the words to make complete sentences. Notice the boldfaced words. Then take turns saying the sentences. Review any words you don't understand.

1 Some anthropologists claim that (love / romantic / of / **notion** / the) is in nearly every culture.

2 Most scientists believe that (**basis** / there / is / **for** / a / biological) feelings of love.

3 One characteristic of people who are in love (is / **attached** / that / are / **to** / they) the object of their love.

4 Romantic people (**to** / the / person / **express** / their / often / **emotions**) they like.

5 People must (love **symbols** / any / with / careful / **of** / be) that they receive.

6 Our brain (**flooded** / many / chemicals / **by** / is) when we fall in love.

7 Specific hormones and chemicals (**in** / **dominant** / **of** / each / are / **phase**) love.

8 Brain chemicals can (**of** / **feelings** / attraction / mutual / enhance) between two people.

9 Our body develops (a / **to** / hormones / some / **tolerance**) over time.

10 There is (the / some / **resistance** / idea / that / **to**) love is determined by brain chemistry.

FOCUS your attention

Lists

Lecturers will sometimes give information in the form of a list. For instance, this could be lists of causes, effects, characteristics, or types of something. These lists are important because they often concern key information in the lecture; thus, this information needs to be a part of your notes if you are to understand the lecture completely and accurately. When adding a list to your notes, be sure to number each item on the list (e.g., 1, 2, 3, etc.).

WAYS LECTURERS INDICATE THEY ARE GOING TO LIST SOMETHING

*Scientists have identified **three causes for** ...*

*There are **four important effects of** ...*

*I would next like to discuss the **three major characteristics of** ...*

*We currently believe that there are **four types of** ...*

A TRY IT Listen to an excerpt from a lecture on three kinds of love. List each kind of love along with its definition. Number each type.

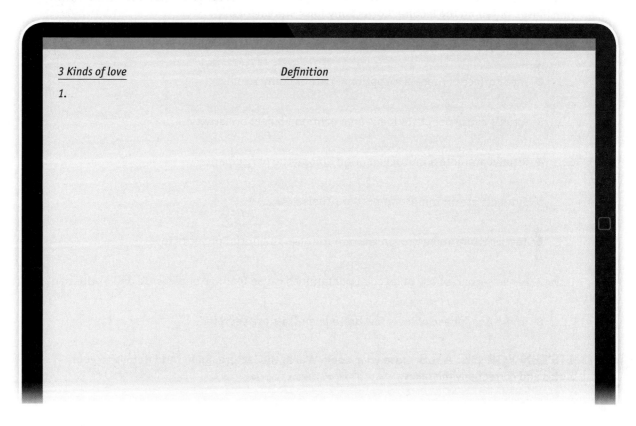

3 Kinds of love   Definition

1.

B PAIR WORK Compare notes with a partner.

WATCH the lecture

A THINK ABOUT IT You are about to watch the unit lecture on the scientific basis of love. The lecturer uses these terms: *romantic, biological, intensity, ritual, objects, symbol, emotional,* and *chemicals*. Think of two sentences she might say, using some of these words.

- _____

_____

- _____

_____

Professor Missy Fox-Brown

B LISTEN FOR MAIN IDEAS Close your book. Watch the lecture and take notes.

C CHECK YOUR UNDERSTANDING Use your notes. Decide if the statements are *T* (true) or *F* (false), based on the lecture. Correct any false statements.

_____ **1** Romantic love has been identified in about half of the world's cultures.

_____ **2** Face-to-face contact is an optional part of many rituals.

_____ **3** Rituals cause people to focus on a common object or activity.

_____ **4** Rituals promote a mutual emotion among the participants.

_____ **5** Symbols are an important part of rituals.

_____ **6** Testosterone and estrogen are important in the initial phase of love.

_____ **7** In the second phase of love, amphetamines cause feelings of pleasure and excitement.

_____ **8** In the final phase of love, few brain chemicals are secreted.

D LISTEN FOR DETAILS Close your book. Watch the lecture again. Add details to your notes and correct any mistakes.

E CHECK YOUR UNDERSTANDING Use your notes. Complete the sentences, based on the lecture.

amphetamines	endorphins	PEA
biologically based	heart-shaped object	ritual
dopamine	oxytocin	testosterone

1 Romantic love is partially _____.

2 A prescribed form of conducting a formal ceremony is a(n) _____.

3 One common symbol of love is a(n) _____.

4 _____ is a hormone that makes people alert to the presence of possible partners.

5 _____ are stimulants that make people feel alert.

6 _____ increases the heart rate and makes people more talkative.

7 _____ is a neurotransmitter that makes people feel euphoric.

8 _____ make people feel a sense of security and calm.

9 _____ is known as the "cuddle chemical" because it produces feelings of attachment to another person.

HEAR the language

Reduced Words and Disappearing Sounds

In natural speech, sounds are sometimes **reduced**, or not clearly articulated—and sometimes they **disappear** entirely. For example, the sounds /t/ and /d/ often disappear if they are followed by a word beginning with a consonant. The phrase *last dance* can be pronounced *lasdance*, and *old boyfriend* as *olboyfriend*. Sounds can also disappear within individual words. For instance, *chocolate* becomes *choclate*, and *vegetable* becomes *vegtable*.

EXAMPLES

Notice the differences between the written and spoken forms:

Written: *In mos(t) cultures marriage is very much a fam(i)ly affair.*
Spoken: *In moscultures marriage is very much a famly affair.*

A LISTEN Listen to the statements from the lecture. In the underlined words, circle the sounds that are reduced or disappear.

1 This suggests that romantic love is at least partly biologically based.

2 For instance, a wedding ring symbolizes a couple's love and commitment.

3 Now let's look at what's happening in your brain and in your body when you feel the emotion that we call romantic love.

4 Recent research indicates that there's a biochemical basis to love.

5 Their brain is literally flooded by hormones and chemicals that cause them to feel the way they feel.

6 We can break the process of falling in love into three fairly distinct phases based on the hormones and chemicals dominant in each phase.

7 In the first phase, the hormones testosterone and estrogen play important roles.

8 It's in the second phase where people have the feeling of being in love.

9 Dopamine has a physical effect on our body—it increases our heart rate and blood pressure.

10 Endorphins are natural painkillers that give us a sense of security and feelings of peace and calm—they basically improve our mood.

B PAIR WORK Practice saying the sentences with a partner. Try to reduce or omit the circled sounds to improve your fluency.

TALK about the topic

Disagreeing

A FOLLOW THE DISCUSSION Watch as the students talk about love. Read each opinion. Then check (√) who agrees with it. More than one student may agree.

River   Hannah   Manny   Mia

	River	Hannah	Manny	Mia
1 Love is the result of a biochemical process.	☐	☐	☐	☐
2 Love isn't completely chemical or hormonal.	☐	☐	☐	☐
3 We can consciously control our feelings.	☐	☐	☐	☐

B LEARN THE STRATEGIES Watch the discussion again. Listen closely for the comments. Check (√) the discussion strategy the student uses.

	Asking for opinions or ideas	Disagreeing	Trying to reach a consensus
1 Hannah: "Who agrees with the idea that love is the result of a biochemical process?"	☐	☐	☐
2 River: "Actually, I don't do much seeking. I'm usually the one being sought."	☐	☐	☐
3 Mia: "I don't think she was saying that."	☐	☐	☐
4 Hannah: "But can we at least agree that we do have some control?"	☐	☐	☐

Discussion Strategy In most conversations, **expressing disagreement** without seeming too disagreeable is key! One way to do so is to first acknowledge the other person's point: *I see what you're saying, but ... .* Or you can be direct: *I simply disagree.* Some people like to soften their position with an apology: *I'm sorry, but ... .* And of course, body language and tone can further shape your message.

C TRY IT In a small group, discuss one or more of these topics. Try to use the discussion strategies you have learned.

- Mia strongly believes that love is the result of biochemical reactions. Do you agree?
- Manny describes his brother and his wife as *content* and *happy*. Is this the highest goal that couples in long-term relationships can aspire to?
- Do you agree with Hannah's belief that people can control their feelings?

REVIEW your notes

REVIEW Read your notes. With a partner, take turns explaining the ideas from the lecture, using the following headings to help you. Then complete these notes together. Be sure the items listed below are numbered in your notes.

4 Characteristics of a ritual

1)

2)

3)

4)

3 Biochemical phases of love

1)

2)

3)

Now you are ready to take the Unit Test and the Proficiency Assessment.

EXPRESS your ideas

Love and Attraction

This unit has focused on biological love. What interests you most about the topic?

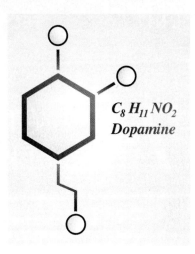

$C_8 H_{11} NO_2$
Dopamine

TASK **Research and give a short presentation on a topic related to love. Keep the presentation management strategies in mind as you prepare.**

Prepare

1 Choose one of these topics:

> Choose a culture you are unfamiliar with. Find out about the way its members express love. Identify ways in which they are similar to and different from those of your own culture.
>
> *Either* read two articles *or* listen to two online audio / video clips that describe current research on the biological basis of love and attraction. Identify information that does not appear in the lecture for this unit and decide which information you found most revealing or intriguing.
>
> Interview your parents or a couple from your own culture and ask: *How did you fall in love? How were you attracted to each other? Why did you decide to get married? Did your love change after you got married?* etc. Describe how attraction, love, and marriage "work" in your culture.

2 As you prepare, try to apply the presentation management strategies.

Practice

3 Practice your presentation with a partner. As you listen to your partner, notice how he or she uses presentation management strategies. Ask two questions to get more details about the topic.

Present

4 Work in groups of 3 or 4. Deliver your presentation to the group. At the end, ask if anyone has any questions or comments.

5 Listen to your group members' presentations.

Evaluate

6 Use the *Unit 6 Presentation Evaluation Form* (in Appendix C) to think about how well your group members managed their presentations.

7 For each presentation, discuss your feedback with the presenter.

Research and Presentation Strategies: Managing your presentation

Good presentation management helps to ensure that your audience will get maximum benefit from your presentation. Not only will it help you to convey your message in the time you have available, it will also help make certain that your audience fully understands that message and the ideas that support it. Here are some tips:

- **Pace your presentation.** Try to organize your presentation into timed information chunks to avoid ending too early and having nothing to say *or* having to squeeze in too much information at the end. For example, you might plan your presentation into six chunks, as follows:

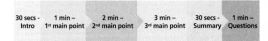

| 30 secs - Intro | 1 min – 1st main point | 2 min – 2nd main point | 3 min – 3rd main point | 30 secs - Summary | 1 min – Questions |

- **Be sensitive to audience attention span.** Remember, people have a fairly short attention span, so try not to dwell on a single point or idea for too long.

- **Handle questions effectively.** Whether you decide to take questions during or after your presentation, allow different people to ask questions and try to spend approximately the same time on each question.

- **Use examples, anecdotes, and analogies to help illustrate ideas.** This will help clarify your ideas, add interest and depth to your presentation, and make your ideas feel more concrete.

- **Be mindful of fluency: rhythm, pausing, intonation.** Using good rhythm, pausing, and intonation makes what you say easier to understand and makes you more interesting and engaging as a presenter.

- **Provide handouts and realia.** Providing handouts and realia is a great way to make presentations more accessible, interesting, and concrete.

7   Artificial Intelligence: The Turning Point

CONNECT to the topic

The computer revolution, digital technology, and new materials have given humankind the tools to achieve things we could only have dreamed of as little as half a century ago. For example, space travel, prosthetic limbs, electronic communication, automated methods of manufacturing, and "intelligent" domestic appliances have changed the way we live as well as what we aspire to as human beings. However, some of these technological developments are disliked, even feared, by some people. This is particularly true of artificial intelligence (AI), where computer systems are able to perform tasks that normally require human intelligence.

A   **THINK ABOUT IT** As a class, list four new technologies that involve artificial intelligence (AI). Then list a reason to fear each.

AI technology	Reason to fear
• _____	_____
• _____	_____
• _____	_____
• _____	_____

B   **TUNE IN** Listen to a discussion with Professor William Mancini about important emerging technologies. Then decide if the statements are *True* or *False*, based on the discussion.

	True	False
1 Applied science technologists search for solutions to real-world problems.	☐	☐
2 Big data is helping shape education.	☐	☐
3 The Network of Things will consist of 150 billion connected objects by 2022.	☐	☐
4 The Network of Things will eventually add $2 trillion to the US economy.	☐	☐
5 Professor Mancini believes scientists are close to creating an intelligent robot.	☐	☐
6 3-D printers have the potential to transform industry.	☐	☐

C   **PAIR WORK** With a partner, discuss one of the technologies mentioned. Think of various ways in which that technology could be beneficial.

LEARNING OUTCOMES

In this unit, you will:

- take organized notes based on a short talk
- recognize main ideas from a technology lecture
- note details from a technology lecture
- identify and practice syllable stress
- recognize and practice asking for opinions or ideas
- discuss the lecture with a partner to prepare for the unit test
- work as a team to present on artificial intelligence (AI) technology

BUILD your vocabulary

A LISTEN The boldfaced words are from the unit lecture on artificial intelligence. Listen to each sentence. Then guess the meaning of the boldfaced word. Work with a partner.

1 The scientific process of developing an intelligent robot is extremely **complex**, involving interrelated fields of research and in-depth tests performed across extended periods of time.

2 The output of a single industrial robot is **equivalent to** that of five human beings, making the robot a highly efficient option.

3 Science fiction movies have led many people to worry about the possible **implications** of robots with real intelligence. In particular, they see them as a possible threat to humankind's very existence.

4 Unlike robots, which are designed to follow a certain logic, human beings do not always behave **rationally**. This can make their behavior difficult to understand and predict.

5 Instead of calmly and intellectually acknowledging both the good and bad points of AI, some people become very **reactionary**.

6 Today's generation can feel much more confident in products that are manufactured using artificial intelligence because these products are much more **reliable**.

7 Some find attempts to **replicate** intelligence and awareness in robots offensive. They believe it's wrong to reproduce these human characteristics in machines.

8 One important human quality that current robots lack is **self-awareness**. They have no "soul" and can only understand and behave according to how they have been programmed.

9 When people see governments developing sophisticated weapons, it's easy to understand why they become **skeptical** about claims that new technologies will be used solely for the good of humankind.

10 Although I support AI, I am a compassionate person and greatly **sympathize with** workers who lose their jobs to robots.

B TRY IT Choose the best definition for each boldfaced word.

1 complex
   a complicated
   b numerous
   c straightforward

2 equivalent to
   a more than
   b less than
   c the same as

3 implications

(a) considerations
~~b~~ consequences
(c̶) threats

4 behave rationally

(a) reasonably
b efficiently
c predictably

5 reactionary

(a) emotional
b negative
c unreasonable

6 reliable

(a) dependable
b simple
c expensive

7 replicate

a please
(b) reproduce
c predict

8 self-awareness

(a) the ability to think about yourself
b the ability to make money for yourself
c the ability to make others notice you

9 skeptical

a certain
b worried
(c) reluctant to believe

10 sympathized with

a thought about
(b) felt sorry for
~~c~~ remembered

C PAIR WORK Cover Group A as your partner reads sentences 1–3. Listen and write the missing words in Group B. Your partner corrects your answers. Switch roles for 4–6.

GROUP A

1 Sci-fi movies often **appeal to** those with an interest in future technology.

2 Workers often dislike the boredom and **monotony of** working on the production line in a factory for many hours, day after day.

3 The **distinction between** ideas in theory and ideas in practice is an important one.

4 Professor Mancini's own research, which includes developing "smart security guards" for office buildings, is **oriented toward** artificial intelligence.

5 The Research Center is interested in the **exploration of** new ideas that can benefit humankind.

6 People's concerns about artificial intelligence are **at odds with** their daily use of intelligent technology.

GROUP B

1 Sci-fi movies often **appeal** _to_ those with an interest in future technology.

2 Workers often dislike the boredom and **monotony** _of_ working on the production line in a factory for many hours, day after day.

3 The **distinction** _between_ ideas in theory and ideas in practice is an important one.

4 Professor Mancini's own research, which includes developing "smart security guards" for office buildings, is **oriented** _toward_ artificial intelligence.

5 The Research Center is interested in the **exploration** _of_ new ideas that can benefit humankind.

6 People's concerns about artificial intelligence are **at odds** _with_ their daily use of intelligent technology.

FOCUS your attention

Organization

Good notes are well-organized notes.

One effective way of organizing your notes is to write the main ideas on the left side of your page and the more detailed, supporting ideas on the right side. There may be a number of different levels of detail, so as your notes move to the right, the level of detail increases. Your notes might look something like this:

(Main idea 1)	
portf intolgence	(Supporting idea 1)
smart computer	(Example 1)
	(Supporting idea 2)
	(Supporting idea 3)
	(Example 1)
	(Example 2)
(Main idea 2)	
	(Supporting idea 1)

A TRY IT Listen to an excerpt of a speaker discussing people's misconceptions about artificial intelligence. Take notes. Try to organize your notes from left to right, based on the main ideas and details you hear.

B PAIR WORK Compare notes with a partner. Can you improve your notes?

WATCH the lecture

A THINK ABOUT IT You are about to watch the unit lecture on artificial intelligence (AI). With a partner, come up with an example of a form of AI that you would welcome in your daily life, and two reasons why.

Professor Helena Sonin

Welcome: _____

_____

Reason 1: _____

_____

_____

Reason 2: _____

_____

_____

B LISTEN FOR MAIN IDEAS Close your book. Watch the lecture and take notes.

C CHECK YOUR UNDERSTANDING Use your notes. Decide if the statements are *T* (true) or *F* (false), based on the lecture. Correct any false statements.

T **1** It's mainly scientists, sociologists, philosophers, and economists who feel strongly about artificial intelligence.

F **2** The introduction of robots into manufacturing was controversial. The reason was because it was expensive.

T **3** Strong forms of artificial intelligence have a kind of real intelligence and are closer to human beings than weak forms.

T F **4** "Technological singularity" is that moment when scientists succeed in creating a truly intelligent robot.

T **5** Artificial intelligence is already providing solutions to global problems.

T **6** Sophisticated AI robots are likely to be more rational than emotional.

D LISTEN FOR DETAILS Close your book. Watch the lecture again. Add details to your notes and correct any mistakes.

E **CHECK YOUR UNDERSTANDING** **Use your notes. Choose the best answer, based on the lecture.**

1 Over time, people tend to _____ new technologies.
a accept   **b** become more suspicious of   **c** reject

2 Most weak AI systems perform _____ .
a two or three tasks   **b** a single task   **c** household tasks

3 The lecturer mentions several sci-fi films to give examples of _____ .
a a weak form of AI   **b** a strong form of AI   **c** classic movies

4 Some people believe that robots will have human levels of intelligence in _____ years.
a 10 or 15   **b** 20 or 30   **c** 10 to 50

5 Two examples of global problems that AI might address are _____ .
a pollution and famine   **b** pollution and climate change   **c** famine and climate change

6 AI robots' lack of emotion means that they won't be able to _____ with humans.
a fall in love   **b** cooperate   **c** sympathize

7 People may begin to _____ if robots take over many of their roles.
a feel useless   **b** accept AI   **c** relax

8 Some believe that creating intelligent robots is morally wrong because it _____ .
a "fools with mother nature"   **b** leaves people without jobs   **c** threatens humankind's existence

HEAR the language

Syllable Stress

Stressed syllables in a word are those syllables that are pronounced longer, louder, and higher in pitch. Placing stress correctly can make the difference between being understood and not being understood, so it's important to get it right.

> **EXAMPLES**
> Remember these rules and examples:
> - In English, it is often the first or early syllables in a word that are stressed: *favorite, happiness, gladly, bigger.*
> - Stress occurs primarily in content words, not function words that carry little meaning. (Function words include prepositions such as *of, at, between;* pronouns such as *he, they, it;* and conjunctions such as *and, while, although.*)
> - Affixes are not normally stressed, except when we might want to emphasize contrast, as in *He was happy not unhappy.* The stress in the word *unhappy* would normally be on the *ha* (*unhappy*).

🔊 **A LISTEN** **Listen to the statements from the lecture. Circle the stressed syllables in the underlined words.**

1 As I promised last time, today I'm going to talk about <u>artificial</u> <u>intelligence</u>.

2 And although this topic has received a lot of <u>attention</u> lately, in fact, AI has always been <u>controversial</u>.

3 <u>Basically</u>, the robots were more <u>efficient</u> and more <u>reliable</u>.

4 Here I'm talking about <u>vacuuming</u> the home, <u>navigating</u> a route, <u>parking</u> your car for you, playing chess against you.

5 They have no <u>awareness</u> of what they're doing and no choice of whether or not to do it.

6 Strong AI is <u>oriented</u> toward creating a thinking, <u>conscious</u> machine that seems to be <u>equivalent</u> to a human being.

7 The AI is <u>developing</u> a <u>meaningful</u>, even <u>overpowering</u> <u>relationship</u>, with their human "masters."

8 Without <u>emotion</u>, an AI robot will not be able to <u>sympathize</u> with individuals and their unique situations—something that's essentially human and which most of us are very good at.

9 Trouble is, although this "<u>freedom</u>" might seem like a good thing, it could also have a <u>downside</u> and lead to feelings of <u>uselessness</u>.

10 Some people believe that intelligence, <u>intuition</u>, and <u>self-awareness</u> are the universe's gift to humankind, and to try to replicate or even improve on them is like "fooling with mother nature."

B PAIR WORK **Take turns saying the sentences with a partner, stressing the circled syllables. Repeat any challenging words.**

TALK about the topic

Asking for Opinions or Ideas

A FOLLOW THE DISCUSSION Watch as the students talk about artificial intelligence. Read each question. Then check (✓) who answers it.

Shelley   Ben   Kenzie   Hugh

	Shelley	Ben	Kenzie	Hugh
1 "What do you mean by 'cool'?"	☐	☐	☐	✓
2 "But you want to be surrounded by intelligent people, don't you?"	☐	☐	☐	✓
3 "Like what? What's an example?"	✓	☐	☐	☐

B LEARN THE STRATEGIES Watch the discussion again. Listen closely for the comments. Check (✓) the discussion strategy the student uses.

	Asking for opinions or ideas	Expressing an opinion	Offering a fact or example
1 **Ben:** "So I think, to me, this whole AI thing is pretty disturbing."	☐	✓	☐
2 **Shelley:** "But it sounds like, Kenzie, you don't feel that way?"	✓	☐	☐
3 **Kenzie:** "Well, like in *2001: A Space Odyssey*. It's kind of an old movie now—but it shows that a robot can make decisions by itself, even if the decision isn't good for humans."	☐	☐	✓
4 **Shelley:** "Any other reasons to oppose AI?"	✓	☐	☐

Discussion Strategy By **asking for opinions or ideas**, you'll not only help others become involved in the discussion, but also enrich the discussion itself. It's as easy as asking, *What do you think?* The next step—listening—is where your learning begins!

C TRY IT In a small group, discuss one or more of these topics. Try to use the discussion strategies you have learned.

- Hugh and Kenzie mention the idea of sci-fi movies predicting the future. What examples can you think of where science fiction has become science fact?

- What are some of the benefits *you* would like to see come from the future development of artificial intelligence?

- What are three examples of literature and film *reflecting* society and three examples of them *shaping* society?

REVIEW your notes

REVIEW In Focus Your Attention (p. 65), you learned to organize your notes more effectively by putting the main ideas on the left and the details on the right. With the help of your notes and the basic outline below, try to reconstruct the lecture with a partner. Add as much detail as possible.

Artificial Intelligence = subject people feel strongly about

AI = historically controversial

2 forms of AI:

Benefits

    2 e.g. of benefits of AI:

Risks

    3 e.g. of risks of AI:

The future?

TIP!

Remember: There are many ways to organize your notes. You can use symbols, like bullets or arrows. Or you might prefer the more formal outline style, with numbers and letters. Choose a style that suits you.

Now you are ready to take the Unit Test and the Proficiency Assessment.

EXPRESS your ideas

The Future Is Now

This unit has looked at artificial intelligence and some of the benefits and risks associated with it. Which new AI technologies are you most excited about?

TASK Research and give a short presentation on the advantages and disadvantages of a new AI technology. Work in pairs or in groups of 3, applying the teamwork strategies.

Prepare

1 Research one of these AI technologies:

3-D printers	Parallella
Eye Tribe	screenless displays
Leap Motion	virtual reality
neurohacking	wireless electricity

2 Include in your presentation what the technology is and some of its advantages and disadvantages.

3 As you prepare, try to apply the teamwork strategies.

Practice

4 Practice your presentation. With your partner or group, consider how well you have implemented the teamwork strategies and discuss how you can improve your presentation.

Present

5 Deliver your presentation to the class. At the end, ask if anyone has any questions or comments.

6 Listen to your classmates' presentations. As you listen to each presentation, write down a question relating to one of the presenter's ideas. At the end of each presentation, ask your question.

Evaluate

7 Use the *Unit 7 Presentation Evaluation Form* (in Appendix C) to think about how well your classmates presented in teams.

8 For each presentation, discuss your feedback with the presenter.

Research and Presentation Strategies: Working as a team

It is quite likely that at some point in your studies or your working life you will be required to prepare and give a presentation with another person or a group. Implementing a few simple strategies can be the difference between a strong performance and a weak one.

- **Decide on roles.** Each person should know exactly what he or she is doing and what his or her responsibilities are. This avoids role confusion and makes the presentation feel more polished and professional.

- **Assign roles according to strengths.** Different people have different strengths. Try to give roles to those who have the skills to perform them best.

- **Introduce all of the presenters.** Introducing yourselves and your roles as presenters is a good practice and helps the audience a) understand the flow of your presentation and b) more easily address questions to particular presenters.

- **Signal switches between presenters.** Your audience will find it easier to follow your presentation if you signal when you are about to switch to another presenter and what that person is going to talk about.

8 Big Brother and the Surveillance Society

CONNECT to the topic

Civil liberties groups argue that in most modern-day societies, the lives of ordinary citizens are no longer private in the way they once were. These groups are concerned that political, commercial, and security organizations now have access to detailed information about us, ranging from our whereabouts to our financial dealings to our personal lifestyle choices. What is particularly worrisome is the fact that many of us are unaware that we are being "watched" in this way.

A THINK ABOUT IT How do you feel about security and being watched? Take this survey. Check (✓) your responses and think of reasons or examples to support them. Then compare with a partner.

	Strongly disagree	Disagree	Agree	Strongly agree
• Security cameras help to reduce crime.	☐	☐	☐	☐
• Security cameras make me feel uncomfortable.	☐	☐	☐	☐
• If I know I'm being observed, I change my behavior.	☐	☐	☐	☐
• I don't mind being watched if it makes society safer.	☐	☐	☐	☐
• Only criminals need to fear police monitoring.	☐	☐	☐	☐
• Too much security threatens our freedom.	☐	☐	☐	☐

B TUNE IN Listen to a conversation with civil liberties expert Gavin Swenson. Then complete the statements, based on the conversation.

1 Governments claim that surveillance exists to keep society _____.

2 Many people are concerned because they feel that surveillance _____ their right to privacy.

3 The National Security Agency's authority to spy on Americans is quite _____.

4 The National Security Agency harvests 40 billion _____ each month.

5 The government also gathers information on _____.

6 An example of phone call metadata may include the _____ of the parties, the _____ of the call, and the _____ of conversation.

C DISCUSS Do you have any experience being watched? Do you care if your personal information is being monitored? What is your opinion about government surveillance? What is your view about individual privacy? Share your ideas with the class.

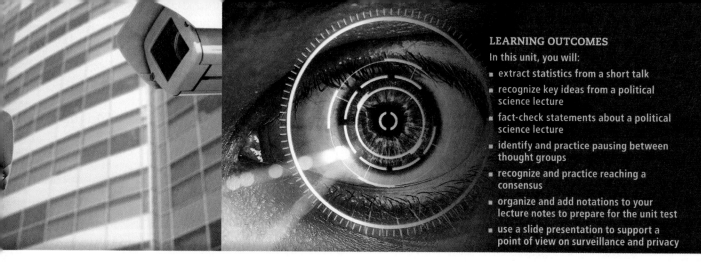

LEARNING OUTCOMES
In this unit, you will:

- extract statistics from a short talk
- recognize key ideas from a political science lecture
- fact-check statements about a political science lecture
- identify and practice pausing between thought groups
- recognize and practice reaching a consensus
- organize and add notations to your lecture notes to prepare for the unit test
- use a slide presentation to support a point of view on surveillance and privacy

BUILD your vocabulary

A LISTEN The boldfaced words are from the unit lecture on surveillance. Listen and complete the definitions.

1 civil liberties: Civil liberties are the _____ and _____ people have in society.

2 commercial: Commercial means having to do with _____ or _____ .

3 composite: Composite means _____ up of _____ _____ or materials.

4 controversial: Something that is controversial causes a _____ of _____ .

5 deterrent: A deterrent is a way of _____ people from _____ something.

6 security: Security refers to _____ taken by agencies to _____ us.

7 sophisticated: If something is sophisticated, it's _____ or _____ .

8 suspected: Somebody who is suspected is _____ to be _____ for doing something _____ .

9 techniques: Techniques are particular _____ or ways of _____ something.

10 via: Via means _____ , by, or _____ way of—for example, "She flew from Prague to New York via London."

B TRY IT Study the words and definitions with a partner, and then test your partner.
EXAMPLE

A: *What are techniques?*

B: *Techniques are ways of doing something.*

C PAIR WORK Cover Column A as your partner reads sentences 1–5. Listen and write the missing words in Column B. Your partner corrects your answers. Switch roles for 6–10.

COLUMN A

1 An important **aspect of** police work is the collecting of criminal evidence.

2 Criminals are carefully **monitored by** police.

3 The boy was **suspected of** theft.

4 Criminals **take advantage of** new technology to commit sophisticated crimes.

5 Security cameras protect us from **threats to** society.

6 We frequently give organizations **access to** our personal details.

7 Some feel that being closely monitored is **the equivalent of** being in prison.

8 Tighter security makes it less likely that we'll be **exposed to** violence in public places.

9 Security cameras have **become part of** normal everyday city life.

10 Many of us are **unaware of** being tracked by security cameras.

COLUMN B

1 An important **aspect** _____ police work is the collecting of criminal evidence.

2 Criminals are carefully **monitored** _____ police.

3 The boy was **suspected** _____ theft.

4 Criminals **take advantage** _____ new technology to commit sophisticated crimes.

5 Security cameras protect us from **threats** _____ society.

6 We frequently give organizations **access** _____ our personal details.

7 Some feel that being closely monitored is **the equivalent** _____ being in prison.

8 Tighter security makes it less likely that we'll be **exposed** _____ violence in public places.

9 Security cameras have **become part** _____ normal everyday city life.

10 Many of us are **unaware** _____ being tracked by security cameras.

FOCUS your attention

Numbers and Statistics

Whether you are studying humanities, social sciences, or physical sciences, you will often work with numbers and statistics.

- Listen carefully for stressed syllables, since many numbers sound similar but have different stress patterns.
- Also, listen for number group markers such as *hundred*, *thousand*, and *million*.
- Finally, note that the word *and* can come before the tens units, although many speakers don't use it.

EXAMPLES

*13 – thir**teen**; 30 – **thirty***
*34,832 – thirty-four **thousand**, eight **hundred** thirty-two*
*256,375 – two **hundred** fifty-six **thousand**, three **hundred** seventy-five*
*18,035,699 – eighteen **million**, thirty-five **thousand**, six **hundred** ninety-nine*
*263 – two hundred (**and**) sixty-three*

A TRY IT Listen to an excerpt from a talk about surveillance cameras in New York City. Note as many statistics as you can.

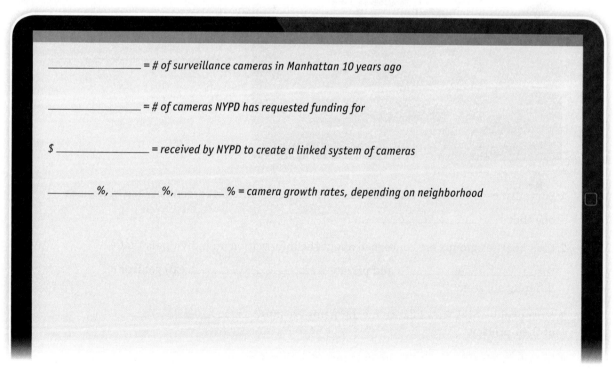

_____ = # of surveillance cameras in Manhattan 10 years ago

_____ = # of cameras NYPD has requested funding for

$ _____ = received by NYPD to create a linked system of cameras

_____ %, _____ %, _____ % = camera growth rates, depending on neighborhood

B PAIR WORK Compare notes with a partner.

WATCH the lecture

A **THINK ABOUT IT** You are about to watch the unit lecture on the increasing use of surveillance systems in the world. List four ways that information about people can be obtained as they go about their day-to-day activities.

- _____
- _____
- _____
- _____

Professor Colin Edwards

B **LISTEN FOR MAIN IDEAS** Close your book. Watch the lecture and take notes.

C **CHECK YOUR UNDERSTANDING** Use your notes. Complete the main ideas, based on the lecture.

300	invasion
credit card	organizations
drones	suspected
facial characteristics	watching
government	

1 Surveillance is the act of carefully _____ a person or place, especially one that's _____ .

2 Civil liberties groups are concerned about the information on individuals that the _____ and private _____ can get from different sources.

3 Most people think surveillance mechanisms are a(n) _____ of their privacy.

4 In Britain, closed-circuit TV cameras record each citizen up to _____ times a day.

5 Some _____ transactions can provide information about where we are and what we are spending.

6 Biometric facial recognition measures _____ .

7 Considered by some to be extravagant toys, _____ are another kind of sophisticated surveillance technology.

🔊 ▶️ **D LISTEN FOR DETAILS** Close your book. Watch the lecture again. Add details to your notes and correct any mistakes.

E CHECK YOUR UNDERSTANDING Use your notes. Decide if the statements are *T* (true) or *F* (false), based on the lecture. Correct any false statements.

_____ 1 Civil liberties groups completely support all uses of surveillance.

_____ 2 Societies where people are monitored a lot are called intrusion cultures.

_____ 3 The number of surveillance cameras in New York City has increased 15 percent in the past few years.

_____ 4 Biometric facial recognition has been used in airports and hospitals.

_____ 5 The portable "trackers" the lecturer mentions extracts data from people's computers.

_____ 6 People are free to use drones as and when they like.

_____ 7 EPIC is probably a civil liberties group.

_____ 8 The lecturer generally appears to support the use of surveillance mechanisms.

HEAR the language

Key Words in Thought Groups

One way to "follow" a speaker more smoothly is to listen for **thought groups** and **key words**. Thought groups are clusters of words that form a single idea in the speaker's mind. Thought groups are separated by pauses, and each thought group usually has one word or phrase that is the "focus." That key word or phrase is usually louder, longer, and has a higher pitch.

> **EXAMPLE**
>
> Notice the thought groups, which are marked with a slash (/), and the key words, which are underlined:
>
> I decided to do an Internet _search_ / and couldn't _believe_ / how many people feel the _same way_ I do / and how many _organizations_ there are / whose _mission_ is / to _fight back_ on this issue /

A LISTEN Listen to the statements from the lecture. Mark the thought groups by adding slashes (/). For each thought group, underline the key word or phrase you hear. Note that punctuation indicating a pause has been removed.

1 Surveillance is the act of carefully watching a person or place especially one that's suspected

2 Today it's possible for savvy private organizations to get information on individuals from different sources and build a kind of composite picture a profile if you will

3 Closed-circuit TV cameras are in stores monitoring shoplifters in cash machines identifying fraud gangs and on public transportation watching vandals and thugs

4 But of course they're also watching perfectly ordinary innocent people like you and me going about their daily lives completely unaware that they're being monitored

5 Right now the UK government is considering recording all car journeys taken on main roads as a deterrent to terrorism and crime generally

6 Every time we use a credit or debit card we're making an announcement of where we are how much we're spending and on what

7 Next up biometric facial recognition which uses computer programs to analyze images of human faces for identification purposes

8 These trackers act as fake cell phone towers allowing police or other government investigators to pinpoint the location of a targeted cell phone by extracting email and other data from it

9 Now drones are small camera-equipped quadcopters basically fancy mini-helicopters you now see them in a lot of places

10 Now I'm no conspiracy theorist but like many people I don't believe all this surveillance is for our own good

B PAIR WORK With a partner, take turns saying the sentences, pausing after each thought group and emphasizing the underlined words.

TALK about the topic

Trying to Reach a Consensus

A FOLLOW THE DISCUSSION Watch as the students talk about surveillance. Read each opinion. Then check (√) who expresses it. In some cases, it may be more than one person.

Ben   Kenzie   Hugh   Shelley

	Ben	Kenzie	Hugh	Shelley
1 It could be difficult to reach agreement on the issue of surveillance.	☐	☐	☐	☐
2 Cameras on and around public transportation are comforting.	☐	☐	☐	☐
3 Surveillance cameras discourage crime in public places.	☐	☐	☐	☐
4 Personal privacy is a human right.	☐	☐	☐	☐

B LEARN THE STRATEGIES Watch the discussion again. Listen closely for the comments. Check (√) the discussion strategy the student uses. More than one answer may be correct.

	Asking for clarification or confirmation	Expressing an opinion	Trying to reach a consensus
1 Kenzie: "I hate the whole idea of surveillance."	☐	☐	☐
2 Hugh: "It's a prevention measure. Is that the right word?"	☐	☐	☐
3 Kenzie: "We all have a right to privacy, don't we?"	☐	☐	☐
4 Ben: "Look, we all feel a bit differently. But is there *any* middle ground—any position we can all agree on?"	☐	☐	☐

Discussion Strategy Getting a group to **reach a consensus**, or agree, can be challenging. One approach is to use questions to identify areas of agreement—for example: *When is everyone free to meet again?* You can follow up by making suggestions based on feedback—for example: *Sounds like Sunday is open for everyone—does that work?*

C TRY IT In a small group, discuss one or more of these topics. Try to use the discussion strategies you have learned.

- What are examples of necessary and unnecessary surveillance?
- Would you prefer to live in a society that has no surveillance and, therefore, possibly less security, or one that has heavy surveillance but is possibly safer?

Big Brother and the Surveillance Society   **79**

REVIEW your notes

Read your notes. Did you write down any numbers or statistics? Explain them to a partner. Then try to reconstruct the lecture, using your notes and the cues below.

Def. of surveillance:

Reasons why civil liberties groups are concerned about it:

5 Surveillance mechanisms + uses:

1. closed-circuit TV cameras:

2. credit cards:

3. biometric facial recognition:

4. cell phone surveillance technology:

5. drones:

The views of
- *the lecturer:*

- *Marc Rotenberg:*

TIP!
Note how decimals, fractions, powers, and square roots are said.

Decimals
4.6 – *four point six*
.04 – *point zero / oh four*

Fractions
1/8 – *one / an eighth*
1/4 – *one / a quarter*
1/3 – *one / a third*
1/2 – *one / a half*
5/8 – *five eighths*
2 1/3 – *two and . . .*

Powers
3^2 – *three squared*
12^3 – *twelve to the third power / twelve cubed*

Square roots
$\sqrt{64}$ – *the square root of sixty-four*
$\sqrt{10}$ – *the square root of ten*

 Now you are ready to take the Unit Test and the Proficiency Assessment.

EXPRESS your ideas

Under the Watchful Eye

In this unit, you have learned about different kinds of surveillance. Do you support or oppose public surveillance? What types of surveillance do you support? What types do you oppose?

TASK Research and give a short presentation on the issues of surveillance and privacy. Include a slideshow.

Prepare

1 Conduct an online or library search for articles supporting and opposing surveillance. Note some of the key arguments that support *your* view. Try to include some of your own arguments.

2 As you prepare, try to apply the slideshow strategies.

Practice

3 Practice your presentation with a partner. Listen to your partner. Give him or her feedback and identify two strengths and two areas for improvement.

Present

4 Work in groups of 3 or 4. Deliver your presentation to the group. At the end, ask if anyone has any questions or comments.

5 Listen to your group members' presentations. As you listen to each presentation, write down a question relating to one of the presenter's slides. At the end of each presentation, ask your question.

Evaluate

6 Use the *Unit 8 Presentation Evaluation Form* (in Appendix C) to think about how well your group members used their slideshows.

7 For each presentation, discuss your feedback with the presenter.

Research and Presentation Strategies: Using slideshows

Today, many people use slideshows to support their presentations. However, using slides effectively is a skill that requires practice. Understanding a few basic principles can help you improve the quality of your presentations.

- **Create a good balance between your voice and the slides.** The slides are not the presentation; they are there to *support* the presentation. It is *you* who should be the *main focus* of the audience's attention.

- **Keep your slides simple.** The slides should include only the key points of your talk—one idea per slide is a good rule to follow. Including too much information makes slides difficult to read and understand.

- **Use visuals.** Slides with too much text are boring. Vary your slides by introducing images and graphics. Visuals can also help your audience understand ideas that may be too complex to explain clearly verbally—for example, a complicated process or the design of a particular technology.

- **Reveal information gradually.** Reveal information on a slide gradually—one point at a time. This way, the audience can absorb the information on the slide along with what you are saying.

9 Animal Communication

CONNECT to the topic

Scientists have long believed that humans can communicate a seemingly infinite number of ideas, while animals can express only rudimentary ideas. But is this actually the case? Animals appear to have far more sophisticated abilities than was once believed. Some researchers now think that in order to unravel the mysteries of animal communication, we must first answer this question: Do humans and animals communicate in the same way?

A THINK ABOUT IT Take this survey about animal communication. Check (✓) your responses and think of reasons or examples to support them. Then compare with a partner.

	Agree	Disagree
• Animals communicate in many different ways.	☐	☐
• Animals can understand what people are feeling.	☐	☐
• Animals can express emotion.	☐	☐
• Animals can use simple words.	☐	☐
• Adult animals teach their young to communicate.	☐	☐
• Animal communication is fundamentally the same as human communication.	☐	☐

B TUNE IN Listen to a discussion with Patrice Waltham about new research on dogs. Then circle the best answer, based on the discussion. Compare answers with a partner.

1 Host Andy Davis thinks dogs are **loyal pets / fun animals /** **good communicators** and great companions.

2 Waltham is a(n) **animal psychic / dog listener /** **animal behaviorist**.

3 The research discussed is about how **humans understand dogs /** **dogs understand dogs /** **dogs understand humans**.

4 When a dog has a negative experience, it wags its tail **to the left /** **to the right / up and down**.

5 The tail-wagging behavior is the result of **training /** **brain structure**.

6 Waltham **is certain /** **unsure** about the value of this research.

C PAIR WORK With a partner, think of possible benefits of understanding animal communication. Identify three benefits. Then share with the class.

BUILD your vocabulary

A LISTEN The boldfaced words are from the unit lecture on animal communication. Listen to each sentence. Then guess the meaning of the boldfaced word. Work with a partner.

1 Gerhard speaks English with a slight German **accent**. His pronunciation is a little different from someone who grew up in an English-speaking country.

2 Every language has many **discrete** sounds. For instance, in English, the *p* in the word *pail* and *t* in the word *tail* are pronounced in different ways.

3 Some animals make meaningful sounds that are **distinct** from one another. For example, a low-pitched sound may communicate anger and a high-pitched sound excitement.

4 Human languages are very **flexible**. People can say the same thing in many different ways.

5 The songs used by older birds are passed on to the younger **generation** of birds. In this way, the young birds learn to sing like their parents.

6 Some chimpanzees have been taught to express an **impressive** number of ideas. Most people are surprised to learn that some chimps understand several hundred words.

7 Dogs express happiness using **nonverbal behavior**. They jump up and down in an excited way and wag their tails quickly.

8 Human communication is fairly **precise**, so we usually understand each other. For example, if you say, "Look at my new hairstyle," I know where to look.

9 Almost all animal communication seems **random** when we look at grammar. Animals seem to use no clear grammar rules.

10 Although some animals can communicate well within their own species, **ultimately**, their ability to communicate with humans is quite limited.

B TRY IT Match each word to the correct definition.

a accent	**d** flexible	**g** nonverbal behavior	**i** random
b discrete	**e** generation	**h** precise	**j** ultimately
c distinct	**f** impressive		

_d_ **1** able to change or be changed easily

_c_ **2** when ideas or things are separate from each other

_f_ **3** when something makes a strong impression or causes admiration

_g_ **4** expressing meaning without words

_e_ **5** a group of people born around the same time

_h_ **6** exact

_a_ **7** the way a person pronounces words

_j_ **8** in the end; finally

_i_ **9** existing in a way that seems to be without reason; unpredictable

_b_ **10** clearly different or separate

Now say each word to yourself. Write _N_ if it is a noun, and _A_ if it is an adjective. Then use each word in a sentence.

____ **1** accent

____ **2** discrete

____ **3** distinct

____ **4** flexible

____ **5** generation

____ **6** impressive

____ **7** nonverbal behavior

____ **8** precise

____ **9** random

____ **10** ultimate

C PAIR WORK With a partner, reorder the words to make complete sentences. Notice the boldfaced words. Then take turns saying the sentences. Review any words you don't understand.

1 Some people (that / **communicate** / they / believe / can / **with**) animals.

2 Animals (**information** / sophisticated / can **convey** / **to** / another / one) using various means.

3 Some animals can express (of / the / **perceptions** / world / their) fairly precisely.

4 The sounds that animals make (past / **to** / not / events / **refer** / do).

5 There is (nothing / **meaning** / the / about / arbitrary) **of** a lion's roar.

6 Both animals and people (of / **range** / use / wide / a) nonverbal behavior.

7 People can produce (**number** / unlimited / sentences / an / **of**) by using the words and grammar of their language.

8 Animals do not (**capacity** / grammar / have / using / **for** / the).

9 Animal communication seems (limited / **compared** / when / very / **to**) human speech.

10 Children (the / are / **at** / acquiring / accent / **skilled**) used in their social community.

FOCUS your attention

Comparisons and Contrasts

In a lecture that includes comparisons and contrasts, it is important to note how items are similar or different.

LANGUAGE USED TO INDICATE SIMILARITIES OR COMPARISONS		
like	*likewise*	*in a similar manner*
in the same way	*as with ... so too with*	*both ... and ...*
as ... as	*not only ... but also*	*parallels*
also	*similar to / similarly*	*in like fashion*

LANGUAGE USED TO INDICATE DIFFERENCES OR CONTRASTS		
but	*more (than)*	*on the other hand*
however	*whereas*	*in contrast*
conversely	*different from*	*unlike*
while	*less (than)*	*although*

One way to contrast two or more items is to note the similarities and differences separately.

Kangaroo rats	Sparrows
• communicate by stamping their feet	• communicate by singing
• ex. "words": "This is mine!" + "Go away!"	• ex. "words": "Above you!" + "Be careful!"

Another way is to note each point of comparison and contrast separately.

	Kangaroo rats	Sparrows
Mode of communication	stamping their feet	singing
Example "words"	"This is my territory!"	"Be careful!"

A TRY IT Listen to an excerpt from a discussion on two modes of animal communication. Take notes and organize them so that the comparisons and contrasts are clear.

B PAIR WORK Compare notes with a partner. Can you improve your notes?

WATCH the lecture

A THINK ABOUT IT You are about to watch the unit lecture on animal communication. List three ways that animals communicate.

Professor Martin Sera

- _____
  _____

- _____
  _____

- _____
  _____

B LISTEN FOR MAIN IDEAS Close your book. Watch the lecture and take notes.

C CHECK YOUR UNDERSTANDING Use your notes. Choose the best answer, based on the lecture.

1 Like humans, animals use both _____ to communicate.
  a sounds and nonverbal communication
  b words and gestures
  c sentences and facial expressions

2 Human communication is _____ than animal communication.
  a older
  b more flexible
  c more direct

3 _____ is defined as the lack of a logical relationship between a sound and its meaning.
  a Arbitrariness
  b Distance
  c Transmission

4 The ability to communicate about things that are not physically present is called _____ .
  a abstraction
  b complexity
  c displacement

5 Bees are able to use dances to communicate information about _____ .
  a their relationship with other bees
  b the presence of enemies
  c the location of a food source

6 The idea that language is passed from one generation to the next is called cultural
  _____ .
  a communication
  b transmission
  c displacement

7 _____ means that language is made up of separate units that can be combined in many ways.
  a Discreteness
  b Phonology
  c Vocabulary

D LISTEN FOR DETAILS Close your book. Watch the lecture again. Add details to your notes and correct any mistakes.

E **CHECK YOUR UNDERSTANDING** **Use your notes. Complete the sentences, based on the lecture.**

accents	distinct meanings	sophistication
arbitrary	grammar	sounds
discreteness	phrases	
displacement	scientists	

1 The growl of an angry dog illustrates that much of animal communication is not

_____ .

2 Meerkats are unusual animals because they are able to use about 20 sounds that

have _____ .

3 Human languages are very flexible because they are made up of a wide range of

_____ .

4 That dogs only express dislike of cats when a cat is present indicates that dogs do not

have the capacity for _____ .

5 The meaning of bee dances is so precise that even _____ can
understand where the food is located.

6 Bee dances provide an excellent example of the _____ of
animal communication.

7 Killer whales are unusual in their ability to pass _____ on to
their young.

8 Chimpanzees have displayed an ability to invent new _____ .

9 Chimpanzees are unable to understand and use _____ in the way that
humans do.

10 Humans have a huge advantage over animals because of the human ability to use

_____ .

HEAR the language

Key Word Stress

Remember that speakers speak in thought groups. Information that is new or that speakers consider most important in a thought group is usually emphasized. Speakers emphasize information by placing **stress on key words**. By stressing some words, the speaker signals to the listener what to pay attention to. Even if you can hear *only* the stressed words, you can often construct the speaker's idea.

EXAMPLES
The underlined words are stressed in these examples:
But do animals <u>really</u> communicate like we do?
Now, the <u>first</u> characteristic we'll look at is <u>arbitrariness</u>.

A LISTEN Listen and complete the statements from the lecture. Underline the stressed words you hear. The number of stressed words is in parentheses.

1 (3) For instance, they convey information to one another, they establish and maintain social organization, and they express their perceptions of the world.

2 (2) Specifically, we'll use four basic characteristics of human language to see how animal and human communication styles compare.

3 (3) But ultimately, we'll see that human communication is far more flexible and better developed.

4 (2) In comparison, a lot of animal communication is not arbitrary.

5 (1) For example, meerkats—a small African animal—can make about 20 distinct sounds.

6 (1) The second characteristic of human language we'll compare is displacement.

7 (4) The meaning of the dance is so clear and so precise that even scientists researching bee dances can interpret exactly where the food is.

8 (2) They live in groups, and different groups develop different accents, just like people.

9 (1) In the use of discreteness, we see that humans have a huge advantage over animals.

10 (4) Discreteness allows us to make complex words and sentences that communicate an unlimited number of meanings, and this is one of the really impressive—actually amazing—aspects of human communication.

B PAIR WORK Practice saying the sentences with a partner, stressing the underlined words. Then discuss why the professor emphasizes the words he does.

TALK about the topic

Expressing an Opinion

A FOLLOW THE DISCUSSION Watch as the students talk about animal communication. Read each statement. Then check (✓) who agrees with it. More than one student may agree.

Hannah   River   Mia   Manny

	Hannah	River	Mia	Manny
1 Animals communicate, and they share some communication characteristics with humans.	☐	✓	✓	☐
2 Animal communication is more sophisticated than we understand.	☐	☐	✓	✓
3 Signaling to other animals isn't using displacement.	✓	✓	☐	☐
4 A meerkat looks like a raccoon.	✓	☐	☐	☐

B LEARN THE STRATEGIES Watch the discussion again. Listen closely for the comments. Check (✓) the discussion strategy the student uses.

	Agreeing	Asking for clarification or confirmation	Expressing an opinion
1 **River:** "Is that what everyone else got from this lecture?"	☐	✓	☐
2 **Mia:** "Pretty much."	✓	☐	☐
3 **Manny:** "But personally, I think animal communication is a lot more sophisticated than we understand."	☐	☐	✓
4 **Mia:** "How so?"	☐	✓	☐

Discussion Strategy In an academic setting, you have numerous opportunities to **express your opinions—** your thoughts, feelings, and positions. But while many opinions start with expressions like *I think, I believe,* and *In my opinion*, only the interesting ones continue with facts, experiences, and other forms of support.

C TRY IT In a small group, discuss one or more of these topics. Try to use the discussion strategies you have learned.

- Manny thinks that animal communication is more sophisticated than most people understand. Do you agree?

- Think of pets you've had or other animals with which you've interacted. Could you detect signs of arbitrariness, displacement, cultural transmission, or discreteness in their communication? Give examples.

- The students give several examples of the complexity of human communication. Can you think of others?

REVIEW your notes

REVIEW Use your notes and the following groups of words to make sentences about the lecture. Write them down. Then with a partner, discuss the main ideas of the lecture using your sentences.

sounds, communicate, verbal behavior, nonverbal behavior

arbitrariness, logical relationship, meaning

humans, flexible, wide range, sounds

displacement, physically present, bees

displacement, humans, books, Internet

cultural transmission, generation, killer whales

discreteness, chimpanzees, combine, phrases

discreteness, humans, combine, words, grammar

Now you are ready to take the Unit Test and the Proficiency Assessment.

EXPRESS your ideas

Connecting with Animals

This unit has focused on animal communication and whether animals can communicate in the same way that humans do. Which animals are you most interested in? What do you know about how they communicate?

TASK **Research and give a short presentation on the communication habits of an animal. Use visual data.**

Prepare

1 Research one animal of particular interest to you. Focus on the following points:

- How it communicates (sounds, scent, body language)

- The animals it communicates with (its own species and other species)

- What meanings it appears to communicate

- An explanation of its communicative behavior in terms of the four points discussed in the unit lecture (arbitrariness, displacement, cultural transmission, discreteness)

2 As you prepare, try to apply the strategies for using visual data.

Practice

3 Practice your presentation with a partner. Listen to your partner. As you listen, notice his or her use of visual data and how effective it is. Make two suggestions for how your partner might improve the use of visual data.

Present

4 Work in groups of 3 or 4. Deliver your presentation to the group. At the end, ask if anyone has any questions or comments.

5 Listen to your group members' presentations. As you listen to each presentation, write down a question you would like to ask concerning the visual data the presenter provided.

Evaluate

6 Use the *Unit 9 Presentation Evaluation Form* (in Appendix C) to think about how well your group members used visual data in their presentations.

7 For each presentation, discuss your feedback with the presenter.

Research and Presentation Strategies: Using visual data

Using visual data—such as pie charts and tables of statistics—is an excellent way to reach your audience. By offering visual support for the ideas you discuss, you make those ideas more understandable and interesting. The following tips can help you decide whether and how to use visual data in presentations:

- **Use visual data to make your presentation more engaging.** Using visual data can make ideas more concrete and bring them to life for your audience.

- **Use visual data for added impact.** Data that is research-based makes your ideas more credible and, therefore, more powerful.

- **Use visuals for abstract topics.** Graphics such as pie charts and creative imagery can help make abstract topics more accessible by giving them greater clarity.

- **Avoid overloading your audience with too much data!** Use just enough data to make your points effectively. Too much data and too much detail can overwhelm your audience and become tiring. The audience will stop paying attention.

- **Make sure your visuals are transparent.** Visual data needs to be unambiguous and easily understood. Be sure your audience understands why you are showing each visual. What idea is it supporting?

10 The Evolution of Money

CONNECT to the topic

Money—every human society uses it. And every modern society needs it in order to grow and flourish. Through the ages, money has had an ability to change in ways that reflect the culture and technology of the time. Shells, cattle, chickens, gold, coins, banknotes, credit cards, open source money, e-money—these are just a few of the many forms that money has taken. And now, for the first time in human history, most of the money that flows throughout the world is not physical; it is digital information that moves over high-speed cables. While the future forms that money will take are hard to predict, one thing is for sure: Money is here to stay.

A THINK ABOUT IT What is your attitude toward money? Take this survey. Check (✓) your responses and think of reasons or examples to support them. Then compare with a partner.

	Agree	Disagree
• It is important to save money every month.	☐	☐
• I prefer to use cash rather than a credit card.	☐	☐
• Having a lot of money is a good thing.	☐	☐
• Money is necessary if we want to help other people.	☐	☐
• I need money to make my dreams come true.	☐	☐
• Money is necessary for a society to grow and develop.	☐	☐

B TUNE IN Listen to an interview with economics professor Dr. Jonathan Pritchard, who discusses the advantages of digital money. Then decide if the statements are *True* or *False*, based on the interview. Compare answers with a partner. Explain what is untrue about the false statements.

	True	False
1 Digital money is usually controlled by a government.	☐	☐
2 Digital money can typically be transferred nearly instantaneously.	☐	☐
3 Personal information remains undisclosed with digital transactions.	☐	☐
4 Different computer codes are used when sending and receiving digital money.	☐	☐
5 The fees for digital transactions are high.	☐	☐

C PAIR WORK Many of our financial transactions do not involve the use of physical money. Do you use physical money or digital money more often? When and where do you use these two types of money? Which do you prefer and why? Discuss with a partner.

BUILD your vocabulary

A LISTEN The boldfaced words are from the unit lecture on money. Listen to each sentence. Then choose the meaning of the boldfaced word.

1 Large cities began to form in Europe as people **abandoned** farmwork and began other kinds of work. They voluntarily moved to urban areas.

  a unable to do something
  b stopped doing something
  c forced to stop doing something

2 Money was originally a concrete object, like gold, but has become increasingly **abstract**. Now some forms of money are a digital computer code.

  a separate from physical realities
  b higher quality
  c valuable

3 Many of the impressive developments we see in modern **civilization** are due to the creation of money. One example is multinational corporations.

  a a large city with many businesses
  b a country with a large population
  c a society in an advanced state of development

4 There are currently many types of **currency** in the world; yen, pesos, dollars, and euros are just a few.

  a stocks
  b precious metals
  c money

5 When money was invented, it provided **enormous** advantages over previous ways of conducting trade. The differences were huge.

  a very gradual
  b completely unexpected
  c extraordinarily large

6 The wealth of rich children is usually tied to **heredity**. Their money often comes from their parents.

  a when a parent encourages a child to work hard
  b when a parent passes on physical possessions to a child
  c when a parent purchases many expensive things for a child

7 When people believe that hard work will be rewarded, individual **initiative** increases dramatically.

    a readiness to take action
    b feelings of tiredness
    (c) the desire to become wealthy

8 The value of money is not **subjective**; the value of one dollar in New York is the same as the value of one dollar in California.

    a changing rapidly and suddenly
    (b) not objective
    c increasing slowly

9 Financial **transactions** involving trillions of dollars take place daily. In the stock market, for example, people exchange shares in hundreds of countries.

    a interactions between sellers and buyers
    b profits and losses
    c putting money into a bank

10 Money has **undergone** tremendous change over the past several thousand years. It now looks very different from the way it once did.

    a caused or created
    b experienced or gone through
    c influenced negatively

B **PAIR WORK** With a partner, reorder the words to make complete sentences. Notice the boldfaced words. Then take turns saying the sentences. Review any words you don't understand.

1 (**role** / positive / played / money / has / a / **in**) billions of people's lives.

2 Money is both physical and digital (**of** / at / this / its / **stage** / evolution).

3 (currency / in / **fluctuations /** values) affect everyone.

4 Paper money (objects / valuable / **symbolic** / **of** / is) such as gold.

5 Money (a / **of** / as / business / **facilitator** / has acted).

6 Attaining wealth was once (almost / **to** / exclusively / heredity / **tied**).

7 Money allowed entire civilizations (**from** / **away** / to / **move**) agriculture.

8 Modern forms of money allow people (with / to / another / business / one / out / **carry**) no matter where they live.

9 Money has been key (the / societies / **of** / modern / **development** / to).

FOCUS your attention

Notations

Taking good notes is one of the first steps to understanding a lecture or presentation. However, it is also important to think about the ideas in the notes. One way of thinking about your notes is to mark them during or after the lecture.

COMMONLY USED MARKING TECHNIQUES
- Underline important ideas.
- Draw stars in the margins to emphasize the most important 5–10 points in the lecture.
- Circle key words and phrases as well as technical vocabulary.
- Draw lines between ideas that have important relationships.
- Write comments to yourself in the margins.
- Write questions in the margins about information that you don't clearly understand.
- Write a short summary statement of the lecture.

The following is an example of how one student marked her notes from a lecture on the influence of money.

What caused them to want independence?

Money led to increases in commerce.

* Businesses gradually developed → ↑ number of people w. $

* People wanted independence, so ...

   - they led the movement toward (democratic values) and gov't.

   - they demanded education for their children

* democratic govts. + more education = more business and commerce

   = a positive (cycle) had begun—we're still in that cycle

Summary: There's a cycle: $ causes commerce to ↑

↑ commerce = ↑ people having $ and this causes society to Δ

e.g., ↑ freedom and ↑ education ... = ↑ $ being earned

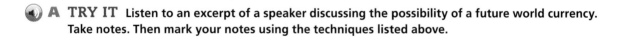

A TRY IT **Listen to an excerpt of a speaker discussing the possibility of a future world currency. Take notes. Then mark your notes using the techniques listed above.**

B PAIR WORK **Compare notes with a partner. Can you improve your notes?**

WATCH the lecture

Professor Alexandra Shaw

A **THINK ABOUT IT** You are about to watch the unit lecture on the evolution of money and the impact of money on society. What are three ways you can pay for goods and services and three ways money influences society?

Ways to pay

- _____
- _____
- _____

Influences of money

- _____
- _____
- _____

B **LISTEN FOR MAIN IDEAS** Close your book. Watch the lecture and take notes.

C **CHECK YOUR UNDERSTANDING** Use your notes. Decide if the statements are *T* (true) or *F* (false), based on the lecture. Correct any false statements.

_____ **1** Barter is a system of direct exchange.

_____ **2** In early societies, landowners possessed most of the wealth.

_____ **3** Money permits people to carry out transactions of any size.

_____ **4** Financial transactions involving money can't be completed quickly.

_____ **5** Money does not move easily across cultural and geographic boundaries.

_____ **6** The value of money is rarely precise.

_____ **7** Money has evolved from being a physical object to an abstract idea.

_____ **8** The rise in commerce was caused by individual initiative.

_____ **9** Money has value independent of the trust and faith that humans place in it.

D **LISTEN FOR DETAILS** Close your book. Watch the lecture again. Add details to your notes and correct any mistakes.

E CHECK YOUR UNDERSTANDING Use your notes. Complete the sentences, based on the lecture.

agriculture	manufactured	precise
brains	more fulfilling	social development
education	paper money	working hard
electronic transactions	physical object	

1 Money can be transferred over any distance in moments using _____ .

2 Money can be used in exact amounts; thus, one major advantage of money is that it is _____ .

3 Originally, money was a(n) _____ found in nature, such as a cow.

4 Barter was replaced by _____ physical objects such as gold coins.

5 Money first became abstract when gold and silver were replaced by _____ .

6 As _____ became more efficient, many people abandoned farmwork and moved to cities.

7 When wealth was no longer tied to heredity, having _____ and _____ became important.

8 The rise of commerce made _____ accessible to more people; this helped new businesses grow.

9 Money is a tool that is related to human and _____ .

10 The creation of money has allowed millions of people to live _____ lives.

HEAR the language

Linking

Spoken English has a rhythm of stressed and unstressed words. Stressed words are emphasized by saying the word louder, longer, and more slowly. Unstressed words are spoken more quickly and are often **linked** together: The final consonant from one word "jumps" to the next word, or the last consonant of one word combines or "assimilates" with the first consonant of the next word. When you are prepared to hear linked sounds, you will be able to understand "fast speech" much better.

Words can be linked when	Spelling	Sounds like
a word ends with a consonant (sound) and the next word starts with a vowel (sound)	*has it*	*ha sit*
	think about	*thin kabout*
	made of	*ma dof*
a word ends with and the next word begins with the same sound	*has some*	*ha some*
	think carefully	*thin carefully*
	made daily	*ma daily*

EXAMPLES
Study these examples of linking sounds across words:

We haven't always used money.
a system of direct exchange
from parent to child
four enormous advantages of money

🔊 **A LISTEN** **Listen and complete the statements from the lecture. Notice how the last sound of the first word links to the first sound of the second word.**

1 Although people could _____ _____ limited business transactions by bartering animals and vegetables, the barter system was _____ _____ fail.

2 The _____ _____ is that financial transactions of any size can take place.

3 For example, _____ _____ for a company to make a transaction involving _____ _____ billions of dollars when using money.

4 And now of course, with electronic transactions, money can be _____ _____ any distance in a flash.

5 Money truly _____ _____ acceptance.

6 OK, let me say a few words _____ _____ evolution of money.

7 Next, money became something more abstract, something that is symbolic _____ _____ objects such as gold and silver.

8 At this _____ _____ its evolution, money became pieces of paper, _____ _____ paper money and stock certificates.

9 These people began to live in cities and to make their livings by offering non-agricultural _____ services.

10 For example, education _____ _____ to many more people.

B PAIR WORK **Practice saying each pair of linked words with a partner. Say them in isolation. Then practice saying the complete sentence, focusing on the linked words.**

TALK about the topic

Agreeing

A FOLLOW THE DISCUSSION Watch as the students talk about the dangers of credit cards. Read each question. Then check (√) who answers it.

Rob   Alana   Ayman   Molly

	Rob	Alana	Ayman	Molly
1 "What happened? Did you lose your card or something?"	☐	☐	☐	☐
2 "How did you find this out?"	☐	☐	☐	☐
3 "So did you have to pay for anything?"	☐	☐	☐	☐

B LEARN THE STRATEGIES Watch the discussion again. Listen closely for the comments. Check (√) the discussion strategy the student uses.

	Agreeing	Expressing an opinion	Offering a fact or example
1 **Ayman:** "It's kind of cool to think that we're seeing money's latest evolution."	☐	☐	☐
2 **Molly:** "Oh, my credit card number got stolen sometime last weekend."	☐	☐	☐
3 **Molly:** "The whole episode has just kind of bummed me out, you know?"	☐	☐	☐
4 **Molly:** "I don't really trust electronic money."	☐	☐	☐
5 **Alana:** "I don't blame you."	☐	☐	☐

Discussion Strategy Observe a group discussion and you're likely to hear **expressions of agreement** like *Uh-huh, Right, Yes!, I agree, Exactly!* and *No doubt.* Agreeing is great way to support another speaker, either to participate in casual conversation or to build an alliance when an issue is being discussed.

C TRY IT In a small group, discuss one or more of these topics. Try to use the discussion strategies you have learned.

- Do you think that cash is safer than credit cards or electronic money?
- Do you think that it is safe to shop on the Internet?
- Would you react similarly to Molly if your credit card number were stolen?

REVIEW your notes

REVIEW Read your notes. With a partner, take turns explaining the ideas from the lecture. Give examples or add comments as you discuss. Then complete the notes below.

- Def. of barter:

- 4 Advantages of money over barter:

  1)

  2)

  3)

  4)

- 3 Ways the invention of money benefited society:

  1)

  2)

  3)

- Description of evolution of money:

Now you are ready to take the Unit Test and the Proficiency Assessment.

EXPRESS your ideas

On the Money

This unit has focused on money, and how it has evolved over time. What changes have you observed personally? How have they impacted your relationship with money?

TASK **Research and give a short presentation on money. Practice answering audience questions.**

Prepare

1 Choose and consider one of these topics:

> Reasons why money is or is not important in your life
>
> Your idea about one aspect of money—for example, how to save money, how to budget your money, how to live on a limited budget
>
> A theory you have about money

Practice

2 Practice your presentation with a partner. Listen to your partner. Ask questions

Present

3 Work in groups of 3 or 4. Deliver your presentation to the group. At the end, ask if anyone has any questions or comments.

4 Listen to your group members' presentations.

Evaluate

5 Use the *Unit 10 Presentation Evaluation Form* (in Appendix C) to think about how well your group members answered audience questions.

6 For each presentation, discuss your feedback with the presenter.

Research and Presentation Strategies: Answering audience questions

Because audience members often wish to ask questions to get additional information or to clarify ideas, an important skill when making a presentation is the ability to answer these questions clearly and concisely. This skill requires knowledge of your topic and the ability to provide information that directly answers the question. Here are five strategies to use when answering questions from the audience:

- **Welcome questions from the audience.** Let audience members know that their questions are welcome by using phrases such as these: *Thank you for the question. That's a good question.* and *That's an important question.*

- **Repeat or rephrase the question.** By repeating the question, you can ensure that you have understood it accurately. This also allows all of the audience members to hear the question clearly.

- **Answer the question directly.** After repeating the question, provide a clear, direct answer. You can then elaborate on your answer by providing additional information.

- **Address your answer to the whole audience.** Although one individual asks a question, your answer is of interest to many people in the audience, so address the entire group when answering the question.

- **Check that you have answered the question adequately.** It is often a good idea to check that you have answered the question satisfactorily by asking, *Did I answer your question?* or *Was my answer clear?*

11 The Fountain of Youth

CONNECT to the topic

Living forever. The possibility has intrigued philosophers, scientists, and novelists for thousands of years. Although living forever is not possible, finding ways to extend the human life span to 100 years and beyond is the object of a great deal of scientific research. To date, the results indicate that it may one day be possible for many people to live well past the age of 100. However, as people live longer, they will have to find a balance between the length and the quality of their lives.

A THINK ABOUT IT Although modern cultures tend to glorify youth, there are both advantages and disadvantages to aging. In a small group, list some of those advantages and disadvantages. Then discuss as a class.

Advantage	Disadvantage
• _____	_____
• _____	_____
• _____	_____

B TUNE IN Listen to a conversation with Dr. Natalie Aldrich about changes in the human life span. Then circle the best answer, based on the conversation. Compare answers with a partner. If they are different, try to agree on the correct answer.

1 A typical life span for much of human history was **30 / 40 / 50** years.

2 The human life span began to become longer at the beginning of the **18th / 19th / 20th** century.

3 On average, the typical life span increases by three **days / weeks / months** every year.

4 Given the current trend, the average American will live to the age of **79 / 88 / 100** in 2050.

5 New medicines have played **no clear role / a minor role / a major role** in increasing the average life span.

6 Dr. Aldrich is confident that the average life span will continue to increase because **it is a stable trend / recent medical breakthroughs have been introduced / researchers will make new discoveries**.

C PAIR WORK List at least three reasons why people might be living longer. Can you think of an unusual suggestion for extending the human life span that you have heard about? Discuss with a partner.

BUILD your vocabulary

A LISTEN The boldfaced words are from the unit lecture on aging. Listen to each sentence. Then circle the meaning of the boldfaced word.

1 Some lifestyles **accelerate** the aging process by damaging the body.

   a increase the speed of something
   b cause something to develop slowly
   c make something easier to notice

2 If our body doesn't get rid of waste products, they will **accumulate** inside our cells. In turn, we can become tired or even sick, and can't function as well.

   a move from one place to another
   b remove
   c gradually increase in quantity or size

3 Scientists—particularly **biologists**—are intrigued by the aging process.

   a people who study living things
   b people who study the natural forces of light and heat
   c people who study the composition of synthetic substances

4 Because a half-cup serving of ice cream typically has 120-plus **calories**, eating too much of it can cause weight gain.

   a large amounts of processed sugar
   b units measuring the amount of energy in food
   c parts of some foods that increase muscle mass

5 Our body is made up of millions of **cells**, with new ones produced daily.

   a tiny organisms that are important to health
   b parts of a person's DNA
   c the smallest parts of a living thing that can exist independently

6 Mice, whose bodies produce extra **electrons**, age faster.

   a heat
   b electricity
   c matter in an atom

7 People with a fast **metabolism** tend to be thin, even if they eat a great deal.

   a an intense type of aerobic exercise
   b the chemical process that changes food into energy
   c the rate at which a person breathes

8 Salt **molecules** are made up of two parts: sodium and chloride.

    a fluids that have become solid

    b the smallest units of matter that have a unique chemical nature

    c the parts of food that give it flavor

9 One benefit of getting proper **nutrition**—including eating protein and a variety of fruits and vegetables—is living a longer life.

    a the balance of food a person consumes

    b food that has not been processed in a factory

    c a diet that does not include any red meat

10 One way to **supplement** our diet is to take vitamins.

    a add something to improve a situation

    b use one thing in place of another

    c simplify something

B PAIR WORK With a partner, take turns completing each sentence with the correct form of the word. Notice the boldfaced words. Read the completed sentences aloud. Review any words you don't understand.

accumulated	accumulating	accumulation

1 _____ evidence indicates that we have the **potential to** control our rate of aging.

2 The _____ of waste products in our cells has a negative **impact on** our bodies.

accelerated	accelerating	acceleration

3 Smoking causes cell damage, and cell damage is **consistent with** _____ aging.

4 One **interpretation of** scientific research is that the _____ **of** our aging process is part of our body's design.

nutrition	nutrients	nutritious

5 Our life span is **affected by** the _____ that are in our food.

6 A diet that restricts caloric intake or cuts out foods **high in** calories can still be

_____ .

FOCUS your attention

Problem-Solution Relationships

In some academic lectures, the speaker's goal is to describe problems and possible solutions to those problems. In this type of lecture, it is important to first clearly distinguish the problems, then determine which solutions apply to which problems.

EXPRESSING PROBLEMS

The first problem is ...

The bad news is ...

This causes problems such as ...

One theory of (the problem) says ...

Think about the implication ...

EXPRESSING REASONS FOR PROBLEMS

The first reason is ...

A second major reason is ...

This is caused by ...

This, in turn, causes ...

This happens because ...

One interpretation is ...

EXPRESSING SOLUTIONS

What can be done about this?

How can we solve this problem?

There is some good news here ...

Is there any good news here?

One possible solution is ...

A TRY IT Listen to an excerpt of a health instructor addressing causes of aging skin and solutions. Take notes. Try to organize your notes so that the problems and their solutions are clearly related.

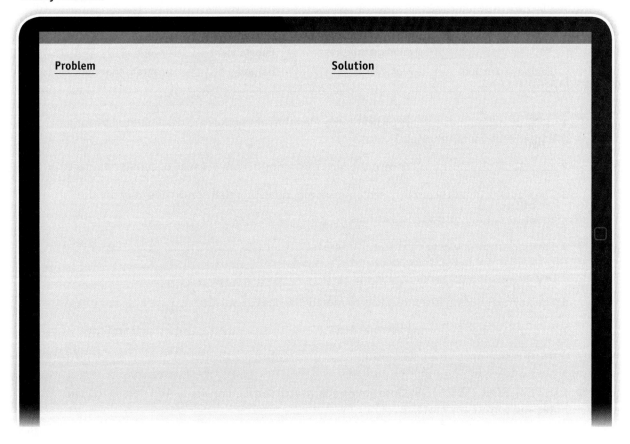

Problem	Solution

B PAIR WORK Compare notes and reactions with a partner. Can you improve your notes?

WATCH the lecture

A **THINK ABOUT IT** You are about to watch the unit lecture on aging. What do you think are the top two causes of aging? What are two ways we might slow the aging process?

Causes

• _____
  _____

• _____
  _____

Professor Emma Gertz

Ways to slow aging

• _____
  _____

• _____
  _____

B **LISTEN FOR MAIN IDEAS** Close your book. Watch the lecture and take notes.

C **CHECK YOUR UNDERSTANDING** Use your notes. Choose the best answer, based on the lecture.

50	damage theories	imbalance	oxygen
calorie restriction	high-tech	natural	program theories

1 _____ are based on the idea that our bodies are designed to live for a limited amount of time.

2 _____ concern the idea that aging occurs because of cellular damage.

3 The Hayflick Limit theory is based on research indicating that some cells only divide about _____ times.

4 The only known way to consistently increase life span is _____ .

5 Free radicals cause aging by creating a(n) _____ .

6 The key to reducing free radicals is to metabolize less _____ .

7 Two approaches to slowing aging are the _____ approach and the _____ approach.

D **LISTEN FOR DETAILS** Close your book. Watch the lecture again. Add details to your notes and correct any mistakes.

E CHECK YOUR UNDERSTANDING Use your notes. Circle the letter of the word or phrase that best completes each idea, based on the lecture.

1 Why were early damage theories incorrect?
  a because damage is not an important cause of aging
  b because damage occurs only temporarily
  c because the human body has the capacity to repair itself

2 What is one interpretation of the Hayflick Limit theory?
  a Our DNA gradually becomes damaged.
  b A cellular clock exists in our DNA.
  c DNA can potentially divide for 50 years.

3 What directly affects the rate of cell division?
  a the amount of waste products in the cell
  b the amount of exercise a person gets
  c the amount of food a person eats

4 By how much should a person reduce his or her caloric intake if the person adopts a CR diet?
  a 20 percent
  b 30 percent
  c 40 percent

5 What is one environmental factor that causes free radicals to form?
  a strong sunlight
  b oxygen
  c air pollution

6 Which of the following is *not* damaged by free radicals?
  a DNA
  b cell membranes
  c electrons

7 What is xenotransplantation?
  a using drugs that reduce the metabolic rate
  b using animal tissues to treat human illnesses
  c using stem cells to repair human organs

HEAR the language

Verb Forms

When you are listening to a lecture, focusing on the verbs will help you understand the main ideas. In addition to hearing the verb, you want to try to understand the basic **verb form(s)**: the tense (present, past, etc.), the voice (active or passive), the mood (imperative-commanding, indicative-stating, conditional, etc.), and whether it's affirmative or negative.

EXAMPLES

Notice the verb forms in these examples:

Most theories of aging fall into just two categories. (present tense, active voice)

Information about our life span is encoded in our DNA. (present tense, passive voice)

Scientists have learned a lot about why we age. (present perfect, active voice)

A LISTEN Listen and complete the statements and questions from the lecture. Then mark the verbs you wrote: present, past, perfect, or future tense; active or passive voice; conditional or imperative mood.

1 Many theories of aging _____ _____ _____ , but most of them fall into just two categories: program theories and damage theories.

2 Program theories say that our bodies _____ _____ to live for a limited amount of time—that information about our life span is encoded in our DNA.

3 This theory _____ _____ in the 1960s by two biologists who

_____ that some cells divide about 50 times, then suddenly stop dividing.

4 The rate of cell division _____ directly _____ by the amount of waste products in the cell.

5 So if we _____ the amount of waste, then the cells _____ _____ more slowly.

6 Also, CR _____ just _____ cell division, it _____ metabolic rate.

7 Now this is potentially important because in mammals, lower metabolic rates _____

_____ with longer life spans.

8 In normal molecules, electrons _____ _____ so that their electrical

energies _____ _____ .

9 So, scientists _____ _____ in the last few decades a lot about why we age, but what can we do about it?

10 Second, _____ _____—or as I mentioned before, _____ your intake of calories by about 30 percent.

B PAIR WORK Practice saying the sentences with a partner. Be mindful of the verb forms.

TALK about the topic

Asking for Clarification or Confirmation

A FOLLOW THE DISCUSSION Watch as the students talk about ways to slow aging. Read each opinion. Then check (√) who disagrees with it. More than one student may disagree.

Hannah   Manny   River   Mia

	Hannah	Manny	River	Mia
1 Everybody knows that the natural approach will slow down the aging process.	☐	☐	☐	☐
2 People don't know what they can do to slow aging.	☐	☐	☐	☐
3 I'd be willing to cut back my diet by 30 percent.	☐	☐	☐	☐

B LEARN THE STRATEGIES Watch the discussion again. Listen closely for the comments. Check (√) the discussion strategy the student uses.

	Asking for clarification or confirmation	Asking for opinions or ideas	Disagreeing
1 Mia: "Huh?"	☐	☐	☐
2 Hannah: "I'm not so sure about that."	☐	☐	☐
3 Hannah: "So what then?"	☐	☐	☐
4 Mia: "... Can I clarify something from earlier in the lecture?"	☐	☐	☐

Discussion Strategy To **clarify** means to make clearer. To **confirm** is to remove doubt. You can clarify or confirm by restating what you understood: *You mean ...* or *Do you mean ... ?* Or you can ask open-ended questions like *What do you mean?* and *Could you clarify ... ?*

C TRY IT In a small group, discuss one or more of these topics. Try to use the discussion strategies you have learned.

- Do you agree with River that the natural approach is the best way to live longer?
- Do you believe that your life span is predetermined?
- Do you agree with Manny's feeling that most people know how to live a healthy life, but don't act on it?

REVIEW your notes

REVIEW Use your notes. Complete the chart with a partner as you discuss the theories and main ideas covered in the lecture.

Theory category	Specific theory	Key terms	Causes of aging—solutions
program theories		cellular waste products metabolic rate	
damage theories		free radicals	

TIP!
Notes that are organized in categories—in a chart, for example—are easier to review. Clean, organized notes can make information more approachable.

 Now you are ready to take the Unit Test and the Proficiency Assessment.

EXPRESS your ideas

Slowing the Hands of Time

This unit has focused on theories of aging, and possible ways to slow down the aging process. Some people "fight" the aging process. Others try to grow old "gracefully." What's your approach to aging?

TASK Research and give a short presentation on slowing the aging process. As you plan, think about how you will create group interactions during your presentation.

Prepare

1 Choose and research one of these topics:

> The life of a person who lived to an exceptionally old age (more than 90). This can be a relative or a person you have never met. Focus on understanding why the person was able to live to such an advanced age.
>
> Some foods that experts believe can help people live longer, and why those foods are so beneficial
>
> A type of lifestyle that is supposed to help people live longer
>
> Your opinion regarding this idea: It is better to live a short life doing what you love than a long life doing what you don't enjoy.

Practice

2 Practice your presentation with a partner. Listen to your partner. Give feedback to your partner about the audience involvement questions and tasks he or she included.

Present

3 Deliver your presentation to the class. Ask the audience members to interact at least two times.

4 Listen to your classmates' presentations.

Evaluate

5 Use the *Unit 11 Presentation Evaluation Form* (in Appendix C) to think about how well your classmates created audience interactions.

6 For each presentation, discuss your feedback with the presenter.

Research and Presentation Strategies: Creating group interactions

A useful technique for giving effective presentations is to ask audience members to interact in small groups at various points in your presentation. This technique can have several benefits including enhancing interest in your presentation, increasing audience involvement in the topic, making your presentation easier to understand, and increasing its impact. Consider these ideas when planning group interactions:

- **Decide on the size of the groups.** For instance, audience members can work together in pairs, small groups of 3 to 4 people, or larger groups of 5 or more.

- **Understand why you are asking audience members to interact.** Reasons may include enhancing interest, increasing involvement, supporting comprehension, and increasing impact.

- **Decide on the questions or tasks you will use.** If you use questions, you should generally ask questions that are thought-provoking and that allow for different answers and perspectives.

- **Consider the timing of the interactions.** You will probably want to "set the scene" in the beginning of the presentation before asking the audience members to interact. You will also want to finish your presentation by summarizing the key points yourself rather than having audience interaction.

- **Decide on how you will respond to the group interactions.** For example, will you ask representative audience members to provide answers to a question, will you provide an answer, or both?

12 Marriage

CONNECT to the topic

Why do people get married? While many people today might answer "for love," the answer to this question is complex. People marry for many different reasons, and many forms of marriage exist in the world. Also, ideas about marriage can change radically in any society over the course of even a single generation. This can be seen in the many ways some parents and children disagree about issues such as who and when to marry, and what type of wedding ceremony to have. Despite all of the complexities, however, one thing seems certain: People will still be getting married for many years to come.

A THINK ABOUT IT Which of these characteristics do you think are most important in a marriage partner? Write your ranking: 1–5 (1 being the most important). Survey two classmates. Then add the numbers and divide by 3 to get the average. Share results with the class.

Characteristic:	Good looks	Kindness	Wealth	Nationality	Intelligence
My rankings:	_____	_____	_____	_____	_____
Classmate A:	_____	_____	_____	_____	_____
Classmate B:	_____	_____	_____	_____	_____
TOTAL / 3 = Average	_____	_____	_____	_____	_____

B TUNE IN Listen to an interview with author Martin Carey about marital relationships. Then circle the best answer, based on the interview. Compare answers with a partner. If they are different, try to agree on the correct answer.

1 Dr. John Gottman's research was based on **detailed statistical analyses / extensive interviews / observations of married couples**.

2 Dr. Gottman's research indicates that good marriages are based on **mutual trust / deep friendship / complete honesty**.

3 According to Carey, successful married couples display **mutual respect for / a liking of / a sense of responsibility for** one another.

4 Successful couples relieve tension by **ignoring each other / being apart / using humor**.

5 Carey says that successful couples **praise one another / correct one another / solve problems together**.

6 Carey implies that unsuccessful couples are **willing to compromise / unwilling to compromise**.

C PAIR WORK In your opinion, what are the three most important ingredients in a healthy marriage? Provide an example for each. Then discuss with a partner.

LEARNING OUTCOMES

In this unit, you will:

■ note personal reactions to topics

■ restate the main ideas of a sociology lecture

■ fact-check statements about a sociology lecture

■ identify and practice introductory phrases

■ recognize and practice offering examples and ideas

■ review and summarize your lecture notes to prepare for the unit test

■ include rhetorical questions in a presentation on an aspect of marriage

BUILD your vocabulary

 A LISTEN The boldfaced words are from the unit lecture on marriage. Listen to each sentence. Then guess the meaning of the boldfaced word. Work with a partner.

1 Most people don't get married until they've reached **adulthood**. Marriages involving children and young teenagers are rare in most parts of the world.

2 Naomi heard that many women are delaying marriage until after they turn 30. She **confirmed** that information by checking the Internet.

3 As people from many countries meet and develop relationships, the number of **interracial** marriages increases.

4 Married couples enjoy a kind of **legitimacy**, while unmarried couples may be considered outside the accepted standards of society.

5 Saed has **matured** a lot since moving out of his parents' house. He's become very responsible and is able to take care of himself.

6 Nationalistic barriers to international marriages are gradually disappearing because meeting someone from a different country is fairly common.

7 One societal **norm** of marriage is that people are expected to marry someone of a similar age. Many people view large differences in age as strange.

8 Growth in the Hispanic **population** in some parts of the United States has caused the number of marriages between Hispanics and whites to rise.

9 One strong reason for marriage in many cultures is a woman becoming **pregnant**. It is important that the child has a father and mother to care for it.

10 My parents are from the same **social class**. They lived in similar neighborhoods, and their parents' incomes were nearly the same.

B TRY IT Match each word to the correct definition.

a adulthood	c interracial	e matured	g norm	i pregnant
b confirmed	d legitimacy	f nationalistic barriers	h population	j social class

_____ **1** when a woman is carrying an unborn offspring in her body

_____ **2** fully developed and behaving in a reasonable way; not childish

_____ **3** a block people face because of their national beliefs

_____ **4** between different races of people

_____ **5** people in a particular area or members of a particular group

_____ **6** determined that something is definitely true

_____ **7** the period of life when a person is completely grown

_____ **8** acceptance, validity

_____ **9** a group of people with a similar rank in society

_____ **10** the usual or acceptable way of doing something

Now say each word to yourself. Write _N_ if it is a noun, _V_ if it is a verb, and _A_ if it is an adjective.

_____ **1** adulthood   _____ **5** matured   _____ **9** pregnant

_____ **2** confirmed   _____ **6** nationalistic barriers   _____ **10** social class

_____ **3** interracial   _____ **7** norm

_____ **4** legitimacy   _____ **8** population

C PAIR WORK With a partner, take turns completing each sentence with the correct form of the word. Notice the boldfaced words. Read the completed sentences aloud. Review any words you don't understand.

confirm	confirmed	confirmation

1 Researchers have _____ that caring for children properly is important to the **survival of** any society.

2 Research showing that married couples are healthier than single people is _____ of the **benefits of** marriage.

legitimate	legitimately	legitimacy

3 Children need to be _____ **linked to** their father.

4 One of the **functions of** marriage is to give the couple _____ in the eyes of society.

mature	maturity	maturation

5 As couples _____, they become **similar to** one another.

6 Greater _____ can result in a **rise in** tolerance toward people of other races.

nations	national	nationalistic

7 The tax policies of _____ governments can provide **pressure for** young people to get married.

8 In most _____, marriages are legally **recognized by** the government.

FOCUS your attention

Personal Reactions to Topics

Taking good notes is a crucial part of understanding a lecture, but it is also important to actively think about the notes.

> **ACTIVE NOTE-TAKING**
> - Add examples from your own life.
> - Agree and disagree with information in the lecture.
> - Suggest an alternative point of view.
> - Consider the implications of information in the lecture.
> - Provide additional reasons for something.
> - Consider the strengths and weaknesses of a position or situation.
> - Predict how the situation will change in the future.

Considering the information in the lecture from various points of view and making a personal connection with that information will help you 1) understand and remember the information better, 2) clarify what you do not understand, and 3) create a more unified understanding of the topic. In short, reacting to the information in your notes is as important as taking high-quality notes.

A TRY IT Listen to an excerpt from a speech discussing marriage in Europe. Complete the notes.

Love and marriage

- A new idea _____

- Up to 300 years ago _____

- People lived and worked _____

Marriage = _____

Economic reason = external motivation for marriage

Internal motivation for marriage = _____

B PAIR WORK Compare notes and reactions with a partner. Then react to the information in your notes by using some of the approaches described above.

WATCH the lecture

Professor David Reed

A THINK ABOUT IT You are about to watch the unit lecture on marriage. Think of two benefits of marriage and two criteria that people use for choosing a marriage partner.

Benefit of marriage

- _____

- _____

Criteria for choosing a partner

- _____

- _____

B LISTEN FOR MAIN IDEAS Close your book. Watch the lecture and take notes.

C CHECK YOUR UNDERSTANDING Use your notes. Choose the best answer, based on the lecture.

1 Some form of marriage exists in _____ .

  a a few societies
  b most societies
  c every society

2 A universal benefit of marriage is that it creates _____ .

  a individual wealth
  b relationships between families
  c social harmony

3 Marriage increases the likelihood that _____ .

  a children will be cared for
  b families will be economically successful
  c society will develop rapidly

4 In most societies, marriage establishes _____ .

  a the parents' legal status
  b the children's caretakers
  c the rights of children

5 Homogamy means that people marry _____ .

  a someone similar to themselves
  b someone chosen by their parents
  c someone only after a long courtship

6 The strongest major trend in marriages of the future is a decline in _____ .

  a religious homogamy
  b racial homogamy
  c educational homogamy

7 Interracial marriages in the United States are increasing because of increases in the

_____ populations.

  a African-American and white
  b Asian and white
  c Hispanic and Asian

🔊 ▶ **D LISTEN FOR DETAILS** Close your book. Watch the lecture again. Add details to your notes and correct any mistakes.

E CHECK YOUR UNDERSTANDING Use your notes. Decide if the statements are *T* (true) or *F* (false), based on the lecture. Correct any false statements.

_____ **1** Anthropologists agree that marriage is the union of two or more people who are legally recognized by the government.

_____ **2** The alliance theory states that marriage increases social cooperation.

_____ **3** Because of the slow development of human children, they need the protection of their parents for a relatively long time.

_____ **4** The legitimacy argument states that a child must be legally linked to his or her mother.

_____ **5** According to the lecturer, 75 percent of Americans marry someone from the same racial group.

_____ **6** Since 1980, the number of interracial marriages in the United States has remained steady.

_____ **7** A recent poll indicated that African Americans showed the greatest acceptance of their grandchildren marrying someone of a different race.

HEAR the language

Discourse Markers

When speaking English, people frequently use **discourse markers** such as introductory phrases to stress information (*Obviously* …), to state a logical relationship (*However*, …), or to lead to a summary (*All right*, …). In all of these cases, the intonation remains level or falls slightly after the introductory phrase and there is a clear pause.

> **EXAMPLES**
> Study these examples:
> *Actually, some anthropologists believe that this is the main reason why marriage developed in human society.*
> *Moreover, children also play a role in the third, and final, benefit we'll discuss.*

A LISTEN Listen and complete the statements and questions from the lecture. Write the introductory words and phrases you hear.

1 _____, most anthropologists, including myself, agree that there is no single definition that adequately describes all of the types of marriages found throughout the world.

2 _____ , some form of marriage is found in every society.

3 _____ , children need parents to care for them for the first few years of their lives.

4 _____, this is quite important to the survival and development of a society.

5 _____, this is known as "the legitimacy argument."

6 _____, I might add that this kind of pressure is lessening in some Western countries.

7 _____ , so I hope that we agree that marriage benefits society in many ways.

8 _____ , more than 90 percent of Americans marry someone from their own racial group, and about 75 percent marry someone from their same social class.

9 _____, why is the phenomenon of homogamy so prevalent?

10 _____ , this trend is accelerating rapidly, and we have many reasons to believe that the number of interracial marriages in the US will continue to increase for some time to come.

B PAIR WORK Practice saying the sentences with a partner. Use level or falling intonation at the end of the introductory phrase, and give a clear pause.

TALK about the topic

Offering an Example or Idea

A FOLLOW THE DISCUSSION Watch as the students talk about modern marriage. Read each anecdote. Then check (√) who identifies with it. More than one answer may be possible.

Michael   Yhinny   Qiang   May

	Michael	Yhinny	Qiang	May
1 I'm used to seeing mixed marriages.	☐	☐	☐	☐
2 My family is conservative.	☐	☐	☐	☐
3 I know a lot of couples who are living together unmarried.	☐	☐	☐	☐

B LEARN THE STRATEGIES Watch the discussion again. Listen closely for the comments. Check (√) the discussion strategy the student uses. More than one answer may be possible.

	Expressing an opinion	Offering an example or idea	Paraphrasing
1 **Michael:** "So in other words, in your parents' generation you see a lot of homogamy, but not in ours?"	☐	☐	☐
2 **Qiang:** "You know what I find fascinating is that in many cultures, marriage seems to be less and less important every day."	☐	☐	☐
3 **Michael:** "Well, I think, even here, generally, couples are expected to get married."	☐	☐	☐
4 **Yhinny:** "I think big changes are ahead!"	☐	☐	☐

Discussion Strategy By **offering an example or idea**, you can transform a topic from theory to reality. This can make the topic not only more understandable, but also more memorable. You can use examples from personal experiences (*In my experience ...*), observations (*I've noticed ...*), and media (*I just read this article in the* Times ...).

C TRY IT In a small group, discuss one or more of these topics. Try to use the discussion strategies you have learned.

- Do you agree with Yhinny that many young couples today are not homogenous?
- Qiang says that "in many cultures, marriage seems to be less and less important every day." How would most people in your community react to this statement?
- How do you think marriage will change in the next 50 years?

REVIEW your notes

REVIEW With a partner, react to these ideas from the lecture. Use your notes and the ideas listed in Focus Your Attention (p. 115) to add comments below. What do you agree or disagree with? Can you add different ideas or reasons? What are the implications of the information in the lecture?

Effects of marriage on social cooperation:

Effects of marriage on child care:

Establishment of children's legal rights:

Marriage partner and social class:

Marriage partner and racial group:

Marriage partner and educational level:

Future of marriage and racial homogamy:

TIP!
Reacting to lecture information and adding those thoughts to your notes is a great practice. You will not only better remember the material, but you will also develop a personal connection to it.

 Now you are ready to take the Unit Test and the Proficiency Assessment.

EXPRESS your ideas

The Perfect Marriage

This unit has focused on the definition of marriage, the benefits of marriage, and the future of marriage. What predictions would you make about marriage?

TASK Research and give a short presentation on an aspect of marriage. Include rhetorical questions.

Prepare

1 Choose and research one of these topics:

> Interview one or two married people about their ideas for making a marriage successful. Report on what you find.
>
> Use the Internet to research interesting marriage customs from around the world. Focus on one area such as food, clothing, or dating customs. Report what you find.
>
> Describe a typical wedding in your community. Discuss aspects of the wedding ceremony that are particularly important and that might be interesting to your audience members.
>
> Interview students about the pros and cons of a couple living together before marriage. Report on what you find.
>
> Interview students about their opinion concerning same-sex marriages. Report on what you find.

2 As you prepare, try to include rhetorical questions.

Practice

3 Practice your presentation with a partner. Listen to your partner. Give feedback to your partner about his or her use of rhetorical questions.

Present

4 Deliver your presentation to the class. Ask the audience at least two rhetorical questions.

5 Listen to your classmates' presentations.

Evaluate

6 Use the *Unit 12 Presentation Evaluation Form* (in Appendix C) to think about how well your classmates used rhetorical questions in their presentations.

7 For each presentation, discuss your feedback with the presenter.

Research and Presentation Strategies: Asking rhetorical questions

A useful technique for giving effective presentations is to ask your audience rhetorical questions at various points in the presentation. A rhetorical question is a question that you ask without expecting an answer. Rhetorical questions help you to involve your audience. The purpose of asking a rhetorical question may be

- to improve audience members' understanding of your presentation.

- to increase your listeners' memory of the information that will follow.

- to encourage the audience to think about the answer.

- to arouse the interest and curiosity of your listeners.

For example, a presenter might ask the audience and then answer the question *What are the social benefits of marriage?* Consider these ideas when planning rhetorical questions:

- **Ask a rhetorical question about key terminology.** One good place to ask a rhetorical question is when introducing key terminology—for instance: *What is the definition of marriage?*

- **Ask a rhetorical question to begin a summary of your main points.** You can begin the conclusion to your presentation by asking a rhetorical question—for example: *So what are the three benefits of marriage we discussed today?*

- **Provide answers to the rhetorical questions you ask.** If you ask a rhetorical question, answer it immediately after asking it. Remember, rhetorical questions don't require your audience to answer them.

APPENDIX A

Academic Word List

Numbers indicate the sublist of the Academic Word List. For example, *abandon* and its family members are in Sublist 8. Sublist 1 contains the most frequent words in the list, and Sublist 10 contains the least frequent. **Boldfacing** indicates that the word is taught in *Contemporary Topics 3*. The page number of the section where the word is taught is indicated in parentheses.

abandon (p. 93)	8	anticipate	9	bulk	9	compile	10
abstract (p. 93)	6	apparent	4	capable	6	complement	8
academy	5	append	8	capacity	5	**complex** (p. 63)	2
access (p. 23)	4	appreciate	8	category	2	component	3
accommodate	9	approach	1	cease	9	compound	5
accompany	8	appropriate	2	challenge	5	comprehensive	7
accumulate (p. 103)	8	approximate	4	channel	7	comprise	7
accurate	6	arbitrary	8	chapter	2	compute	2
achieve	2	area	1	chart	8	conceive	10
acknowledge	6	aspect	2	**chemical** (p. 43)	7	concentrate	4
acquire (p. 33)	2	assemble	10	circumstance	3	concept	1
adapt	7	assess	1	cite	6	conclude	2
adequate	4	assign	6	**civil** (p. 73)	4	concurrent	9
adjacent	10	assist	2	clarify	8	conduct	2
adjust	5	assume	1	classic	7	confer	4
administrate	2	assure	9	clause	5	confine	9
adult (p. 113)	7	**attach** (p. 53)	6	code	4	**confirm** (p. 113)	7
advocate	7	attain	9	coherent	9	conflict	5
affect	2	**attitude** (p. 3)	4	coincide	9	conform	8
aggregate	6	attribute	4	collapse	10	consent	3
aid	7	author	6	colleague	10	consequent	2
albeit	10	authority	1	commence	9	considerable	3
allocate	6	automate	8	comment	3	**consist** (p. 13)	1
alter	5	available	1	commission	2	**constant** (p. 3)	3
alternative	3	**aware** (p. 63)	5	commit	4	constitute	1
ambiguous	8	behalf	9	commodity	8	constrain	3
amend	5	**benefit** (p. 103)	1	communicate	4	**construct** (p. 3)	2
analogy	9	bias	8	community	2	consult	5
analyze	1	bond	6	compatible	9	consume	2
annual	4	brief	6	compensate	3	contact	5

contemporary	8	despite	4	ensure	3	fluctuate	8
context	1	detect	8	entity	5	focus	2
contract	1	deviate	8	environment	1	format	9
contradict	8	device	9	equate	2	formula	1
contrary	7	**devote** (p. 13)	9	equip	7	forthcoming	10
contrast	4	differentiate	7	**equivalent** (p. 63)	5	found	9
contribute (p. 23)	3	dimension	4	erode	9	foundation	7
controversy (p. 73)	9	diminish	9	error	4	framework	3
convene	3	**discrete** (p. 83)	5	establish	1	**function** (p. 103)	1
converse	9	discriminate	6	estate	6	fund	3
convert	7	displace	8	estimate	1	fundamental	5
convince	10	display	6	ethic	9	furthermore	6
cooperate	6	dispose	7	ethnic	4	gender	6
coordinate	3	**distinct** (p. 83)	2	evaluate	2	**generate** (p. 23)	5
core	3	distort	9	eventual	8	**generation** (p. 83)	5
corporate	3	distribute	1	evident	1	globe	7
correspond	3	**diverse** (p. 43)	6	**evolve** (p. 3)	5	goal	4
couple (p. 113)	7	document	3	exceed	6	grade	7
create	1	domain	6	exclude	3	grant	4
credit	2	domestic	4	**exhibit** (p. 13)	8	guarantee	7
criteria	3	dominate	3	**expand** (p. 3)	5	guideline	8
crucial	8	draft	5	expert	6	hence	4
culture	2	drama	8	explicit	6	hierarchy	7
currency (p. 93)	8	duration	9	exploit	8	highlight	8
cycle	4	dynamic	7	export	1	hypothesis	4
data	1	economy	1	expose	5	identical	7
debate	4	edit	6	external	5	**identify** (p. 3)	1
decade (p. 43)	7	element	2	extract	7	ideology	7
decline	5	eliminate	7	facilitate	5	ignorance	6
deduce	3	emerge	4	factor	1	illustrate	3
define	1	emphasis	3	feature	2	image	5
definite	7	empirical	7	federal	6	immigrate	3
demonstrate	3	enable	5	fee	6	impact	2
denote	8	encounter	10	file	7	implement	4
deny	7	energy	5	final	2	**implicate** (p. 63)	4
depress	10	enforce	5	finance	1	**implicit** (p. 43)	8
derive	1	**enhance** (p. 53)	6	finite	7	imply	3
design	2	**enormous** (p. 93)	10	**flexible** (p. 63)	6	impose	4

incentive	6	investigate	4	minimal	9	parallel	4
incidence	6	**invoke** (p. 53)	10	minimize	8	parameter	4
incline	10	involve	1	minimum	6	participate	2
income	1	isolate	7	ministry	6	partner	3
incorporate	6	issue	1	minor	3	passive	9
index	6	item	2	mode	7	perceive	2
indicate (p. 23)	1	job	4	modify	5	percent	1
individual	1	journal	2	monitor	5	period	1
induce	8	justify	3	**motive** (p. 13)	6	persist	10
inevitable (p. 3)	8	label	4	**mutual** (p. 53)	9	perspective	5
infer	7	labor	1	negate	3	phase	4
infrastructure	8	layer	3	network	5	**phenomenon** (p. 3)	7
inherent	9	lecture	6	neutral	6	philosophy	3
inhibit	6	legal	1	nevertheless	6	physical	3
initial	3	legislate	1	nonetheless	10	**plus** (p. 103)	8
initiate (p. 93)	6	levy	10	**norm** (p. 113)	9	policy	1
injure	2	liberal	5	normal	2	portion	9
innovate	7	license	5	notion	5	pose	10
input	6	likewise	10	notwithstanding	10	positive	2
insert	7	link	3	nuclear	8	**potential** (p. 23)	2
insight	9	locate	3	objective	5	practitioner	8
inspect	8	**logic** (p. 43)	5	**obtain** (p. 23)	2	precede	6
instance	3	maintain	2	obvious	4	**precise** (p. 83)	5
institute	2	major	1	**occupy** (p. 33)	4	predict	4
instruct	6	**manipulate** (p. 43)	8	occur	1	**predominant** (p. 13)	8
integral	9	manual	9	odd	10	preliminary	9
integrate	4	margin	5	offset	8	presume	6
integrity	10	**mature** (p. 113)	9	ongoing	10	previous	2
intelligence (p. 33)	6	maximize	3	option	4	primary	2
intense	8	mechanism	4	orient	5	prime	5
interact	3	media	7	outcome	3	principal	4
intermediate	9	mediate	9	output	4	principle	1
internal	4	medical	5	overall	4	prior	4
interpret	1	medium	9	overlap	9	**priority** (p. 33)	7
interval	6	mental	5	overseas	6	proceed	1
intervene	7	method	1	panel	10	process	1
intrinsic	10	migrate	6	paradigm	7	professional	4
invest	2	military	9	paragraph	8	prohibit	7

project	4	respond	1	stable	5	thesis	7
promote	4	restore	8	statistic	4	topic	7
proportion	3	restrain	9	status	4	trace	6
prospect (p. 53)	8	restrict	2	straightforward	10	tradition	2
protocol	9	**retain** (p. 43)	4	**strategy** (p. 13)	2	transfer	2
psychology (p. 43)	5	reveal	6	stress	4	transform	6
publication	7	revenue	5	structure	1	transit	5
publish	3	reverse	7	style	5	transmit	7
purchase	2	revise	8	submit	7	transport	6
pursue	5	revolution	9	subordinate	9	trend	5
qualitative	9	rigid	9	subsequent	4	trigger	9
quote	7	role	1	subsidy	6	**ultimate** (p. 83)	7
radical	8	route	9	substitute	5	**undergo** (p. 93)	10
random (p. 83)	8	scenario	9	successor	7	**underlie** (p. 13)	6
range	2	schedule	8	sufficient	3	undertake	4
ratio	5	scheme	3	sum	4	uniform	8
rational (p. 63)	6	scope	6	summary	4	unify	9
react (p. 63)	3	section	1	**supplement** (p. 103)	9	unique	7
recover	6	sector	1	survey	2	utilize	6
refine	9	**secure** (p. 73)	2	survive	7	valid	3
regime	4	seek	2	suspend	9	vary	1
region	2	select	2	sustain	5	vehicle	8
register	3	sequence	3	symbol	5	version	5
regulate	2	series	4	tape	6	**via** (p. 73)	8
reinforce (p. 3)	8	sex	3	target	5	violate	9
reject	5	shift	3	task	3	virtual	8
relax	9	significant	1	team	9	visible	7
release (p. 43)	7	similar	1	technical	3	vision	9
relevant	2	simulate	7	**technique** (p. 73)	3	visual	8
reluctance	10	site	2	technology	3	volume	3
rely (p. 63)	3	so-called	10	**temporary** (p. 43)	9	voluntary	7
remove	3	sole	7	tense	8	welfare	5
require	1	somewhat	7	terminate	8	whereas	5
research	1	source	1	text	2	whereby	10
reside	2	specific	1	theme	8	**widespread** (p. 3)	8
resolve	4	specify	3	theory	1		
resource	2	sphere	9	thereby	8		

APPENDIX B

Affix Charts

Learning the meanings of affixes can help you identify unfamiliar words you read or hear. A *prefix* is a letter or group of letters at the beginning of a word. It usually changes the meaning. A *suffix* is a letter or group of letters at the end of a word. It usually changes the part of speech. The charts below contain common prefixes and suffixes. Refer to the charts as you use this book.

PREFIX	MEANING	EXAMPLE
a-, ab-, il-, im-, in-, ir-, un-	not, without	atypical, abnormal illegal, impossible, inconvenient, irregular, unfair
anti-	opposed to, against	antisocial, antiseptic
co-, col-, com-, con-, cor-	with, together	coexist, collect, commune, connect, correct
de-	give something the opposite quality	decriminalize
dis-	not, remove	disapprove, disarm
ex-	no longer, former	ex-wife, ex-president
ex-	out, from	export, exit
extra-	outside, beyond	extracurricular, extraordinary
in-, im-	in, into	incoming, import
inter-	between, among	international
post-	later than, after	postgraduate
pro-	in favor of	pro-education
semi-	half, partly	semicircle, semi-literate
sub-	under, below, less important	subway, submarine, subordinate
super-	larger, greater, stronger	supermarket, supervisor

SUFFIX	MEANING	EXAMPLE
-able, -ible	having the quality of, capable of *(adj)*	comfortable, responsible
-al, -ial	relating to *(adj)*	professional, ceremonial
-ence, -ance, -ency, -ancy,	the act, state, or quality of *(n)*	intelligence, performance, competency, conservancy
-ation, -tion, -ion	the act, state, or result of *(n)*	examination, selection, facilitation
-er, -or, -ar, -ist	someone who does a particular thing *(n)*	photographer, editor, beggar, psychologist
-ful	full of *(adj)*	beautiful, harmful, fearful
-ify, -ize	give something a particular quality *(v)*	clarify, modernize
-ility	the quality of *(n)*	affordability, responsibility, humility
-ism	a political or religious belief system *(n)*	atheism, capitalism
-ist	relating to (or someone who has) a political or religious belief *(adj, n)*	Buddhist, socialist
-ive, -ous, -ious,	having a particular quality *(adj)*	creative, dangerous, mysterious
-ity	a particular quality *(n)*	popularity, creativity
-less	without *(adj)*	careless, worthless
-ly	in a particular way *(adj, adv)*	briefly, fluently
-ment	conditions that result from something *(n)*	government, development
-ness	quality of *(n)*	happiness, seriousness

APPENDIX C

Student Presentation Evaluation Forms for Express Your Ideas

Use these forms to evaluate your classmates' presentations.

UNIT 1

EVALUATION FORM: Conducting effective research

1 - Strongly Disagree, 2 - Disagree, 3 - Agree, 4 - Strongly Agree	1	2	3	4
ORGANIZATION The focus of the presentation was clear.				
CONTENT The information provided was relevant to the topic.				
PREPARATION The topic was sufficiently researched.				
DELIVERY The presenter's own voice was evident.				
AUDIENCE INVOLVEMENT I felt interested and involved in the presentation.				

Total: _____

Suggest how the person might improve his or her techniques for future presentations. List 3 points.

1 _____

2 _____

3 _____

UNIT 2

EVALUATION FORM: Considering your audience

1 - Strongly Disagree, 2 - Disagree, 3 - Agree, 4 - Strongly Agree	1	2	3	4
ORGANIZATION The presentation was well organized and easy to follow.				
OPENING The presenter explained the structure of the presentation.				
CONTENT The presenter explained important ideas and / or terminology.				
VALUE I learned something new from the presentation.				
AUDIENCE INVOLVEMENT I felt interested and involved in the presentation.				

Total: _____

Suggest how the person might improve his or her techniques for future presentations. List 3 points.

1 _____

2 _____

3 _____

UNIT 3

EVALUATION FORM: Practicing

1 - Strongly Disagree, 2 - Disagree, 3 - Agree, 4 - Strongly Agree	1	2	3	4
FLUENCY The presenter spoke fluently.				
NATURALNESS The presenter sounded natural.				
CONTENT The presenter gave some new and insightful ideas.				
AUDIENCE INVOLVEMENT The audience seemed engaged and interested in the topic.				
PREPARATION The presentation seemed to have been practiced enough.				

Total: _____

Suggest how the person might improve his or her techniques for future presentations. List 3 points.

1 _____

2 _____

3 _____

UNIT 4

EVALUATION FORM: Giving an organized presentation

1 - Strongly Disagree, 2 - Disagree, 3 - Agree, 4 - Strongly Agree	1	2	3	4
OPENING The presenter previewed the main ideas in the beginning of the presentation.				
ORGANIZATION One main idea was developed in each "paragraph."				
TRANSITIONS Topic changes were clear and easy to follow.				
CONTENT The key points were clear and easy to understand.				
CLOSING The presenter reviewed the main ideas at the end of the presentation.				

Total: _____

Suggest how the person might improve his or her techniques for future presentations. List 3 points.

1 _____

2 _____

3 _____

UNIT 5

EVALUATION FORM: Connecting with your audience

1 - Strongly Disagree, 2 - Disagree, 3 - Agree, 4 - Strongly Agree	1	2	3	4
ORGANIZATION The introduction and conclusion were interesting.				
DELIVERY The presenter appeared confident.				
CONTENT The information provided was relevant to the topic.				
AUDIENCE INVOLVEMENT The presenter was attentive to the audience members.				
VALUE I felt a connection with the presenter.				

Total: _____

Suggest how the person might improve his or her techniques for future presentations. List 3 points.

1 _____

2 _____

3 _____

UNIT 6

EVALUATION FORM: Managing your presentation

1 - Strongly Disagree, 2 - Disagree, 3 - Agree, 4 - Strongly Agree	1	2	3	4
PACING The presentation was well paced.				
ORGANIZATION I was able to follow the presentation easily.				
AUDIENCE INVOLVEMENT I felt comfortable about asking questions.				
INFORMATION VALUE The amount of information was about right for the length of the presentation.				
SUPPORT The handouts / realia increased the clarity and interest of the presentation.				

Total: _____

Suggest how the person might improve his or her techniques for future presentations. List 3 points.

1 _____

2 _____

3 _____

UNIT 7

EVALUATION FORM: Working as a team

1 - Strongly Disagree, 2 - Disagree, 3 - Agree, 4 - Strongly Agree	1	2	3	4
CLARITY The identities of the presenters were made clear.				
ORGANIZATION The presenters worked fluently together and seemed well organized.				
FOCUS It was clear to me what each presenter was focusing on.				
TEAMWORK I could understand when and why speakers switched between each other.				
DELIVERY Each presenter seemed comfortable and confident in his or her role.				

Total: _____

Suggest how the person might improve his or her techniques for future presentations. List 3 points.

1 _____

2 _____

3 _____

UNIT 8

EVALUATION FORM: Using slideshows

1 - Strongly Disagree, 2 - Disagree, 3 - Agree, 4 - Strongly Agree	1	2	3	4
SUPPORT The slideshow supported rather than dominated the presentation.				
COMMUNICATIVENESS The slides were easy to read and contained key information.				
VALUE The slides featured helpful visuals.				
PACING Information was revealed gradually.				
CONTENT The slideshow enhanced the presentation.				

Total: _____

Suggest how the person might improve his or her techniques for future presentations. List 3 points.

1 _____

2 _____

3 _____

UNIT 9

EVALUATION FORM: Using visual data

1 - Strongly Disagree, 2 - Disagree, 3 - Agree, 4 - Strongly Agree	1	2	3	4
SUPPORT The visual data was easy to read and understand.				
CONTENT The presenter's visual data made it easier for me to follow the ideas.				
IMPACT The visual data made the presentation more powerful.				
COMPLEXITY The presentation contained the right amount of visual data.				
CLARITY The presenter clearly explained the visual data.				

Total: _____

Suggest how the person might improve his or her techniques for future presentations. List 3 points.

1 _____

2 _____

3 _____

UNIT 10

EVALUATION FORM: Answering audience questions

1 - Strongly Disagree, 2 - Disagree, 3 - Agree, 4 - Strongly Agree	1	2	3	4
RECEPTIVENESS The presenter welcomed questions from the audience.				
CLARITY The presenter repeated or rephrased questions.				
DIRECTNESS The presenter answered questions directly and clearly.				
AUDIENCE INVOLVEMENT The presenter addressed answers to the whole class.				
CONFIRMATION The presenter checked that questions were answered adequately.				

Total: _____

Suggest how the person might improve his or her techniques for future presentations. List 3 points.

1 _____

2 _____

3 _____

UNIT 11

EVALUATION FORM: Creating group interactions

1 - Strongly Disagree, 2 - Disagree, 3 - Agree, 4 - Strongly Agree	1	2	3	4
ORGANIZATION The presenter "set the scene" and gave us a purpose for interacting.				
MANAGING THE GROUP The size of the groups (pair, small group, large group) was appropriate for the interaction.				
AUDIENCE INVOLVEMENT The group interactions increased my interest and involvement in the presentation.				
CONTENT The group interactions improved my comprehension of the presentation. The timing of the group interactions was appropriate.				
RESPONSIVENESS The presenter made good responses to the group interactions.				

Total: _____

Suggest how the person might improve his or her techniques for future presentations. List 3 points.

1 _____

2 _____

3 _____

UNIT 12

EVALUATION FORM: Asking rhetorical questions

1 - Strongly Disagree, 2 - Disagree, 3 - Agree, 4 - Strongly Agree	1	2	3	4
CONTENT The presenter's rhetorical question helped me understand key terminology.				
ORGANIZATION The presenter's rhetorical question helped me understand the main points.				
SUMMARIZATION The presenter gave answers to his or her rhetorical questions.				
DELIVERY The presenter's eye contact made me feel involved in the presentation.				
PRONUNCIATION The presenter's tone of voice made me feel involved in the presentation.				

Total: _____

Suggest how the person might improve his or her techniques for future presentations. List 3 points.

1 _____

2 _____

3 _____

Notes and Assignments

Photo Credits

Pages 2–3 ARENA Creative/Shutterstock; **Page 3** Jenkedco/Shutterstock; **Page 7** Tatiana Kostenko/Shutterstock; **Page 11** SoleilC/Shutterstock **Pages 12–13** XY/Fotolia; **Page 13** BillionPhotos/Fotolia; **Page 17** Cherries/Fotolia; **Page 21** Cheryl Casey/Shutterstock **Pages 22–23** Rawpixel/Fotolia; **Page 23** PureSolution/Shutterstock; **Page 27** Andrey Popov/Shutterstock; **Page 31** Rawpixel/Shutterstock **Pages 32–33** Rawpixel/Shutterstock; **Page 33** Rawpixel/Shutterstock; **Page 37** Golden Pixels LLC/Shutterstock; **Page 41** Astro System/Fotolia **Pages 42–43** Lucian Milasan/Fotolia; **Page 43** Andrey Kuzmin/Fotolia; **Page 47** Gorillaimages/Shutterstock; **Page 51** Soul wind/Fotolia **Pages 52–53** Nuvolanevicata/Fotolia; **Page 53** Pedrosala/Shutterstock; **Page 57** Nolte Lourens/Shutterstock; **Page 61** Mikael Miro/Fotolia **Pages 62–63** Tatiana Shepeleva/Shutterstock; **Page 63** Benny Marty/Fotolia; **Page 67** Olga Serdyuk/123RF; **Page 71** William Andrew/Photographer's Choice RF/Getty Images **Pages 72–73** Kuzma/Shutterstock; **Page 73** Peshkova/Shutterstock; **Page 76** (bottom): Paul Fleet/Shutterstock; **Page 77** RHIMAGE/Shutterstock; **Page 81** Rena Schild/Shutterstock; **Pages 82–83** Ammit Jack/Shutterstock; **Page 83** Aedkafl/Fotolia; **Page 87** Defpicture/Shutterstock; **Page 91** Rostyle/Fotolia **Pages 92–93** Monticellllo/Fotolia; **Page 93** Menna/Shutterstock; **Page 97** Tyler Olson/Fotolia; **Page 101** Bopav/Shutterstock **Pages 102–103** Dragon Images/Fotolia; **Page 103**: Mountain Inside/Fotolia; **Page 107** Mopic/Shutterstock; **Page 111** Lord and Leverett/Pearson Education, Inc. **Pages 112–113** Jayakumar/Shutterstock; **Page 113** Oralz/Fotolia; **Page 117** IVY PHOTOS/Shutterstock; **Page 121** Phaendin/Shutterstock